Dear Myra, Dear Max

A conversation about aging

By
Myra F. Levick
and Maxine Borowsky Junge

Dear Myra, Dear Max is a book about growing older by a 93 year-old woman (Myra) and an 80 year-old woman (Max). It is an epistolary book–an email conversation of close to four years in which two women of different generations and different living situations–Myra lives in an Independent Living community and Max lives alone with her dog Betsy–share their thoughts about their lives and ponder the big questions of meaning that plague everyone who is alive and thinks. Despite health issues, we kept writing. Originally, we were motivated because we couldn't find anything to read about people 75 plus years old that seemed pertinent to us and was anything but myths, assumptions and opinions. Exploring, we learned how little literature at all there was about this age group and how it was pretty much limited to the "it's not as bad as all that, but old age is not for sissies" department with a tad of inspirational stuff thrown in. One large national study included a few "older" people, but told stories about at retirement now, how so many were able to create new careers of what they "really wanted to do" all along. There is no question people are living longer and as Baby Boomers encounter retirement age, more attention is being paid.

Perhaps ageism will eventually come more to the forefront and the aging become visible and valued as they should be. We hope so. But there are those of us even older than Baby Boomers who are real social pioneers trekking along a path with few landmarks or touchstones to guide the way. In this book you will find out a lot about us. Frankly, we hope some of it will be helpful and that at least you know you are not alone. A few days ago, a friend responded to an email I'd sent by writing "Congratulations on refusing to retire!" I sent her back an email that said "This is what retirement looks like these days." We hope you enjoy our book.
Love,
Myra and Max

DEAR MYRA, DEAR MAX
A Conversation About Aging

ISBN-13: 978-1974444427

ISBN-10: 1974444422

Cover Image by Myra F. Levick, 2017
Cover Design by Ahna Dunn-Wilder

DEDICATION

To all those 75 plus year olds who live with wisdom, generosity, humor and a sense of tomorrow while making every day count. They are creating history as they go.

Age doesn't matter much unless you are a cheese

–Billie Burke

Old age is too often self-inflicted...Most things break, including hearts. The lessons of a life amount not to wisdom but to scar tissue and callus.

...There is a feeling part of us that does not grow old at all. If we could peel off the callus...there we would be, untouched by time, unwithered, vulnerable, afflicted and volatile and blind to consequence...

–Wallace Stegner

Every loss diminishes one's life–and somehow redoubles one's responsibility

–Fritz Stern

FOREWORD
By Myra's Daughters:
Bonnie Cossrow, Karen Gomer and Marsha Levick

This book is a much needed dialogue about growing older between two very intelligent women, both pioneers in their shared profession of Art Therapy, who are experiencing aging in two very different ways. On opposite coasts, they are 13 years apart in age and live in very different circumstances. One is in her own home, living independently with her dog. The other is in an independent living facility with approximately 200 other people, mostly singles, and with about ten couples. Despite their age difference–80 and 93, both women are astute and cognizant of the circumstances they find themselves in, and are able to critique their individual experiences with commentary that is relevant and fascinating to readers of any age. There is specific information for their aging peers as they navigate their situations and environments, respond to their communities, and adjust to their changed lifestyles due to aging and circumstance.

There is also useful information here for anyone involved in developing or delivering services to the elderly– what is needed, what is missing, what works, what can be improved. And there is useful information for their children and for the generations that follow. These writers offer keen insights and an understanding of what seniors' experience as they age–their joys, heartaches, challenges, and losses. Importantly, they manifest that the very best way to hear this message is to engage in dialogue with the elder population –and to **listen**.

On a bittersweet note, how poignant it is that these two old friends were able to bridge thousands of miles to share, enlighten, rejoice and grieve together. This lively and extensive exchange is a needed spotlight on a process that is too often shrouded in mystery, and a testament to a special friendship that brings that experience into the light.

Bonnie Cossrow lives in Boca Raton, Florida and is a retired psychologist.

Karen Gomer lives in Boynton Beach, Florida and is a retired art psychotherapist and exhibiting artist.

Marsha Levick is the Deputy Director and Chief Counsel for the Juvenile Law Center in Philadelphia, Pennsylvania.

FOREWORD
By Max's Children:
Alexa Junge and Benjamin Junge

We think we know our parents. They raised us after all. And yet, all too often there are blind spots in what we know about our parents' professional lives. When we think back on our own mother's career, we remember a woman who built and directed a graduate program in clinical art psychotherapy at Loyola Marymount University in Los Angeles, who inspired a devoted following of students, who published prodigiously, and who maintained a private psychotherapy and art therapy practice. Actually, we remember a lot, and we've always admired our mother's tireless devotion to her field, to her program, and to her students. (She also managed to be an attentive and present mom in our lives while she was juggling such a demanding professional career!)

But there's a lot we didn't know—that, as she writes in the Introduction, children can't ever really know—and for us one of the many pleasures of this book has been that it has taught us something new about our mother. This book is a reminder that behind the academic work—the teaching, the research, the publications and presentations, and clinical practice—are living, breathing people who respect and help each other, challenge and argue with each other, and in different ways love each other.

The long correspondence this book encapsulates, reveals a friendship that until well into Mom's retirement we barely knew existed. And despite being a friendship of the long-distance variety (it has been years since Max and Myra last saw each other in person), the e-ruminations these two smart, passionate women have shared have been important for each of them. There is a mutual respect, playfulness, and interest in the hum-drum of everyday life that we find very moving, which remind us how important Mom's ties of friendship with professional colleagues across the country (and indeed, around the world) have been over the years.

We've always admired our mother's deep passion for social justice, but this book's conversations remind us how concerns about justice and inequality in the U.S.—the election of a Black president, for example—were never peripheral to her work as a pioneer in art therapy, (or to her own work as a gifted visual artist) but instead have always been at the core of her professional identity and commitment.

Reading through Max and Myra's correspondence, we're hardly surprised these two women like each other. They certainly have a lot in common: Both have been architects of the field of art therapy, building graduate programs that today remain among the best in the country. But in addition to their work "on the inside," both women have advocated and agitated, sharing in these pages their stories of indignation and struggles to nudge the field of art therapy (and social justice in the US) in the right direction.

Mom's friendship with Myra, of course, has taken shape during the "late" phase of both women's careers. Indeed, it is primarily since Mom retired and re-settled to Whidbey Island that the email correspondence has really taken off. For us, then, there is something poignant about the parallel between the maturing of the field of art therapy and our mother's entry into her life's eighth decade. This is naturally a bit scary to us (80!) but also inspiring—We are in awe of Mom's drive and remarkable productivity as a person in so-called "retirement."

Finally, this book elicits feelings of gratitude. We are very grateful to Myra, who has obviously been an inspiring figure to our mother—a trailblazer who in her own way has helped Mom find and develop her own place and voice in American Art Therapy. We're also deeply appreciative of the new vantage point this book affords from which to know and love our mother—the vantage point of an enduring friendship, a personal and professional project of visionary sculpting of art therapy in the United States and sisterly solidarity.

Alexa Junge is a TV and movie writer and producer and a playwright. She lives in Los Angeles.

Benjamin Junge is Associate Professor of Anthropology at SUNY in New Paltz where he is also Director of the Latin American Studies Program and does research in Brazil. He lives in Beacon, New York.

DEAR MYRA, DEAR MAX

Table of Contents

INTRODUCTION

Maxine Borowsky Junge

In 1992, doing research for my first book *A History of Art Therapy in the United States,*[1] I went to read the archives of the American Art Therapy Association (AATA), the professional association for art therapists in this country. They were then in a cardboard box at the Menninger Foundation in Topeka, Kansas. Sitting on the dusty floor, I read through all the old letters and other material leading to the founding of the Association in 1969 and Myra Levick emerged as my hero from all that personal, written rancor and conflict. In those old letters, I read of Myra's consistency and steadiness, her grace and generosity and realized that without her, the American Art Therapy Association and my career as an art therapist probably wouldn't have happened at all. Myra was one of AATA's founders and its first President and therefore arguably is responsible–almost totally, I'd say–for the flourishing of art therapy in America.

---

[1] Published in 1994 by the American Art Therapy Association, it was the first history of the establishment of art therapy in the United States.

Myra and I got to know each other first as art therapy colleagues and found that we generally shared a level of anger about how things were going. Twenty-five years later I wrote *The Modern History of Art Therapy in the United States*[2] and asked Myra to write a Foreword for the book, which she did beautifully.

I came to know Myra in a different way after her husband, Len, suddenly died and she almost as suddenly, it seemed to me, moved to live in an Independent Living facility in Florida. I had moved too, retiring as a professor from Loyola Marymount University I went from Los Angeles to Whidbey Island, Washington. Leaving the freeways and noise of Los Angeles where I had been born, by then cemented over, I came to live in the relative rural serenity of Whidbey Island, Washington.

So from the two far coasts, our emails to each other began to express our views about aging that we were both undergoing, if differently. I found that Myra had a sharp, insightful and at times righteously angry mind which I

---

[2] Published in 2010 by Charles C Thomas, Publisher, Ltd., it supplants, expands and contextualizes the first book and brings the history up to date. It remains the only one of its kind and is used in art therapy education programs across the United States.

appreciated. Eventually we began to think about this book together.

Myra and I have known each other for about 50 years but the last 20 or so have been all email. We haven't seen each other "in the flesh" in decades. I want to acknowledge here how much her support and friendship have meant to me through the years. Despite the best of intentions, children don't really understand. Many would like to, but they don't. Perhaps one of the important lessons of this book is that it's wonderful to have a buddy as one ages.

In our preliminary steps, we checked out what was already done on "Seniors"[3] as they were called and, given the fact, that U.S. society is rapidly aging and living longer, found there was surprisingly little research and writing on the post 75 population.

At that time, there were a number of humorous books, generally making fun of the stereotypic "symptoms" of aging and trying to say aging is funny, yes, but not necessarily bad. *Old is not a four-letter word* is one of this genre. What research there was seemed to stop at age 75. For example, in one particular study by Sarah Lawrence

---

[3] We have been looking for a better designation than "Seniors." Lynn Willeman calls post 75 people "Classics."

Lightfoot, *The third chapter*, a large nationwide sample was interviewed and researched, but the stories in the resulting book tended to be about close-to-fifty-sixty year olds retiring and then starting new careers of what they "really wanted to do" all the time. More recently published has been large-scale longitudinal research which says things like seniors with social interactions live longer[4]. Atol Gawande's wonderful book *Being mortal* taught some truths about aging and death that for a variety of reasons had not been recognized by much of anybody, certainly not the medical profession. There is also *Jimmi Hendrix turns 80* by Tim Sandlin published in 2007, a novel about a group of old hippies in an Assisted Living facility in San Francisco who protest and revolt. (Sounded like they were thinking about the nuanced implications of aging even then, although it was from the author's imagination.)

When I went to school in the early 1970s to become a psychotherapist, the life-span theoreticians defined the task of this "last" developmental stage (which, as I recall, started then in the 60s,) as "Life Review." In other words, the main thing there was for seniors growing older to do was *look back and remember*. They live in their memories and

---

[4] Author's note: Some do, some don't.

in the past, said the theorists. The future no longer exists in this last act, they said. Even then, that didn't seem to be right to me. I also remembered that the great developmentalist Erik Erikson first ended his stage theory about age 50. It was only when he himself began to age, that he added some further stages.[5] Myra and I became aware that we were in the land of assumptions and myths,– assumptions and myths often held as *truths.*

People are living longer these days and having vital and enriching lives for many years. I believe "seniors" are social pioneers who may have a tough time seeing their reflections in the writings about them so far and in the world. There isn't much. This book, *Dear Myra, Dear Max* then is an email dialogue between two post-75-year-old women. (Myra is 93 now and I will turn 80 in August 2017). It contains descriptions and thoughts and feelings about our two different lives–Myra lives in an Independent Living facility and I live alone with my dog Betsy (mostly happily) in a house overlooking Puget Sound in Washington state. The book will probably be humorous at times and it will

---

[5] Now, Erickson's 8th and final stage of psychosocial development– 65-end of life– posits the crisis of Integrity vs Despair. The senior looks back and evaluates whether she or he lived a meaningful life. If so, the developmental crisis resolves as "Integrity." If not, it resolves as "Despair." Baloney!

probably be sad. Most of all it will be *true* as we see it and true as we have experienced it. We do not pretend to be "everywoman," but we intend here an honest consideration of our own experiences and our thoughts about aging and it is our hope that this book may speak to others as they traverse this largely uncharted path.

Myra F. Levick

In August of 2011, I suddenly and unexpectedly became a widow. I was 87 years-old that month and my husband, Len, would have been 90 years old; We would have celebrated our 68th anniversary in four months. When it happened, we were in relatively good health, active socially, still driving and requiring no help in maintaining ourselves and our home. One evening, shortly after going to bed, Len woke suddenly, said he was having difficulty breathing and I must call 911. Four days later, just hours after acquiring a pacemaker he suffered a massive coronary and passed away.

Once the planning, the funeral and the event to celebrate Len's life as a respected and loved oncologist, a beloved husband, father, grandfather and great grandfather were over, I was confronted with deciding my single future. I knew I could not remain alone in our apartment in a country club area in southern Florida. Each of my three daughters and sons-in laws invited me to live with them. But my final decision was inspired and informed by the model of my mother who had died in her sleep, at 95, in a nursing home. At that time there were no Independent or Assisted

Living communities but she was very clear about not wanting to live with any children. When she was in need of nursing care, she made the decision to enter a nursing home close to where we lived which was where she finally died. She was wheelchair bound but fortunately, for her and our family, never developed dementia and she amazed us all with her ability to adjust and to participate in whatever she could.

And so, I told my children I would be looking at Independent living communities. In November of that year, 2011, I moved into a lovely, small apartment overlooking a lake at an Independent Living facility, not far from my former neighborhood where I still had a number of friends. But I confess, after five years here, I am still "adjusting." I find moving away from old friends, meeting new people at this age, especially living alone, is a challenge, an adventure and a new experience every day.

As an author and an art psychotherapist, I realized I had so many thoughts about living here, responses and reactions from family and friends I had to put them down on paper. And the idea for this book was born. I shared these thoughts with a dear friend and colleague, Dr. Maxine Junge, younger than I by 13 years, divorced and living independently in her own house. As we wrote to each other, shared our daily experiences, we realized we were collaborating and needed to write a book together. In this process we have learned that aging itself is a challenge and adventure and, as it is said, "not for sissies." In the pages that follow, we share those challenges, our responses, our high moments and our low moments and what we are still learning about getting old.

QUOTES BY FRIENDS

Just turned 87. I think I am in pretty good shape for the shape I am in.
  – Frank Rose, Age 87

With sadness, there is gladness.
  – Jean Goldberg, age 93

Years ago I heard a Zen Roshi say "When your toe hurts you become your toe. You are now your toe." Well, I refuse to become my hip, or my foot or my knees or my toe. So I think I'll just continue to become my next project instead.
  – Diane Divelbess, age 82

Many of us have achieved great goals in life. But perhaps reaching old age is the greatest goal of all.
  – Jack Kulick, age 93

Make art, write, do something creative to savor life twice.
  – Fara Wexler, age 88

I never thought I would get old. I also never thought I would be as strong, as knowledgeable, or as resilient as I turned out.
  – Carolyn Yarnes Woolston, age 80

Drink a little good wine every day and you will live longer.
  – Joe Weinberg, age 99, wine merchant

Aging is a bundle of life's complexities all wrapped up in a creaky body that doesn't suit the passionate ebbs and flows. It is every past age I have lived through—cocked, loaded and firing at odd moments. It is worthy work and not one-bit boring.
  – Wendy Miller Lambeth, age 75

Old age is not for old people.
  – the late Teddi Shallan, age 78

Stay busy with life. Keep your M & Ms (mind and mobility) alive and well. Look forward to the rest of your life.
  – Paul Duben, age 92

Over 75. Stunningly obvious path to wild success: taking the step—making the call—throwing out the invitation—really listening, really connecting—sending the email—opening the book—writing the words, the paragraph, the essay, letter, postcard—attending the lecture, workshop, course, theater, film—entering the studio—putting on Tyvek suit, hat, mask gloves—opening the bag of clay—consulting the ideas file—visiting the friend, gallery, museum—putting on the walking shoes, swimsuit, party outfit, pjs—starting to drive.
  – Inge Roberts, age 77

Perhaps we are not meant to know. Perhaps we must ultimately learn to live with the uncertainty of our ending...to find satisfaction in the smallest things and in the present because the past is gone and the future is unknown. This takes great courage...which we don't often attribute to elders.
  – Fara Wexler, age 88

PART I

2013 & 2014

November 10, 2013

Dear Max,

I am still not done with my NLAPW [National League of American Pen Women] task. It has become much more than I ever anticipated and would certainly have been better if my co-chair had not resigned because of illness. I learned that in this organization, the chair of the nominating committee has full responsibility to prepare the slate. I was confronted with a candidate who was incompetent for the position she applied for and I had to have her withdraw or be withdrawn. It was not nice. It is done, I think, and I just need to write my report.

For self-therapy, I started checking out library books for us from the West Wing Library (here's a link.) I looked over it and saw nothing like what we want to do, but will go back and read more carefully and check more library lists.

Hope all is good with you.

Love,

Myra

JOURNAL

Maxine Borowsky Junge

November 26, 2013–Tuesday

Went to yoga class this am. Those exercises usually make my hip problems feel better. Certainly, the calm I feel and the lack of "pushing" are good for me. And I know that slowly, slowly it is making me stronger. I like to refer to myself as "the skeptic who will try anything" and most of those things such as acupuncture (which I have tried) I consider—like my dead brother the M.D., snake oil. But I know that yoga works—it has for me before and even lowered my blood pressure.

Home now. My housekeeper was here this am and the house always looks and feels good when she has been here. It is quiet, the heat is going and running up the electric bill and I have the humidifier going in my bedroom. I just got it a few days ago, hoping that it will help my eyes hurt less. My son, Ben in NY, says he uses his for six months a year for his sinus problems. My hurty eyes were diagnosed in the summer as allergies and with no organic other reason—so eye drops and hot washcloths. This did help, but I hoped the problem would go away when fall came. It didn't. The weather has been very cold and sunny and they still hurt and run—so I have to assume it is yet another charming indication of old age. Is it what they used to call "rheumy eyes"? Where did I hear that? I need to look out for the aches and pains being too big in my life and limiting it too much, although a certain amount of that at 76 is inevitable, I guess. During a mini-epiphany last week, I determined to take more pain meds as needed, do more exercises—I have been pretty pain avoidant—and to not let it take over my life. Easy to say when feeling less pain. We'll see. I am to go on a small-boat cruise in January with my friend Virginia. The boat should be fine, but I am worried about the plane trip to Miami and St Thomas, sitting all that time and felt at one point, I shouldn't have been so fool hardy as to sign up for it. I have had a chair moved into my bedroom corner and try to sit in it and watch TV a few hours a day–otherwise I would lie on my bed. I have a sense that when I do that, my hip and leg may constrict and even hurt more. Of course, I'll probably never know and the various docs have no idea–people 75+ these days are real social pioneers, in all areas. What is written and often considered "true" is simply based on prevalent cultural assumptions. And you can't believe the internet. Not many years ago, everyone said that all older people do is look back and "life review." As my doc Susan said in response to some research or other about social/friend connections making older people live longer: "They didn't ask introverts!" Probably didn't. Probably couldn't find them.

So now I sit comfortably at my computer, catching up and eventually beginning work on my other book about students becoming art therapists. As I was beginning to wake up this morning, with the window blinds and my eyes shut in my bedroom, not wanting to leave the delicious warmth of the bed and electric blanket, I heard the "boop, boop" of the ferry in Puget Sound—a sure sign that it was foggy. I like the fog—it seems fuzzy and cozy and soft. My daughter Alexa called early this am as I was just getting up. She said "Nobody is dead" when I said that people didn't call at that hour unless there was an emergency. When I told her about one of the "Real housewives of Atlanta" who had named her recent baby "Mr. President" she asked whether his first name was Mister and were they getting ready to do "Real housewives of WHIDBEY."

Love,

Max

November 19, 2014

Dear Myra,

Good and quiet here. Verrrry cold. Rain coming. Cortisone for my hip helping but still hurting. Going to get a second opinion with a fancy doc in Seattle. Couldn't hurt. Happy Turkey Day!

Love,

Max

November 19, 2014

Dear Max,

I hope all is well on the west coast. It is suddenly freezing here.

I really planned for this book to be light and hopefully funny–and I have some funny stories–but I realize there's a flip side too, and the equal part is the losing of people from your everyday life.

The cold weather is not good for arthritis and I am feeling it. I walk through open corridors from one building to another. I have some notes I have been keeping about our book, however the past two weeks have been very sad for me and others here. The only woman I could call a dear friend–a friend I made shortly after I moved in–has been dying from cancer for well over a year and finally gave in and went to Hospice. Her loving granddaughter flies in from Milwaukee every weekend. She died Friday and there will be memorials in her church and here on Saturday. Her granddaughter asked me to write something and when she read what I wrote, she asked that I read at both memorials. It certainly gives an overview of living in a community of 80-100 year olds and facing so many losses.

Love,

Myra

November 20, 2014

Dear Myra,

I want our book to be "true" with the good, the funny, the bad–and certainly loss is a major issue. I am going to start keeping these emails between us. Perhaps they will go in the book!

Oh Myra, I'm so sorry about your friend. I loved your tribute, but imagine the memorials will be difficult to get through. I'm not planning to have one when the time comes. As they say, it dredges up everything–uggg.

In her later years, when my mother's friends began dying, as her then 40-year old daughter, I didn't know how she could stand it. So sad. But now I have decided it may be an additional developmental stage of *acceptance.* A major difference between you and me, is that living as you do, you are close to so many "older" people, and death sometimes is the inevitable outcome. For example, a dear old friend of mine died recently and while I will miss him, we didn't live together and he was not part of my everyday life. And I do remember when somebody I disliked intensely, who had been awful to me and to many others, died finally–I cheered!

As I think of it, independent/assisted living etc. is an interesting format for older people, one in which they are bound to experience a lot of loss. Are we supposed to practice getting used to loss? I wonder how much loss is "good" or "healthy" for people, if we can even call it that. A friend of mine said recently: "I'm trying not to let loss limit my life." Atol Gawande in *Being Mortal* has something to say about this–that older people need *meaning* in their life, not simply a safe environment. What do you think?

Drawing? When I came to Whidbey, I promised myself I would never do any art or art therapy teaching. I looked around for an uninstructed drawing group which, as you know, is ubiquitous most places. Not so here. So I finally gave in and, with an old friend, started one.

We pay for the model and draw. We meet weekly and usually have enough money left over to cater lunch for our last meeting before summer. We have been going for about 9 years now.

It is mostly older people, because we meet during the day. We talk sometimes and share stories, but it is essentially a working group–mostly women, although we have had a few men and have two "regulars" now. One young man was in the navy in Oak Harbor. He took the bus down the island–about an hour–and said he wanted to learn to draw so he could go to art school. (I still hear from him occasionally, from Texas.) Another man, when he was deciding whether to come or not asked if "the hens" were still there.

And we have been together for nine years and that means we are all nine years older, so as the organizer I have to take that into consideration–forgetting things more for some.

Love,

Max

November 22, 2014

Hi Max,

The memorials are over and they were difficult. And as I passed through the lobby on my way in, I was stopped with a request to go to an apartment tomorrow after 12:30– another cohort died suddenly yesterday, funeral tomorrow, reception after in her apartment. I planned to paint this afternoon but just couldn't bring myself to change and go to the art room. I took a nap instead and went to dinner. We have entertainment every Saturday night–most mediocre, some really bad, and a few really good. Tonight was excellent, but it did not really help cheer me up much. But it is my only night activity with a sweet neighbor. And it does keep me out until 8pm–Whoopee!

Your [drawing] class sounds good and something we need to do. For years after Len and I moved to Florida, I attended painting and watercolor classes set up by the art museum for artists. No instructor, just space and ability to use fee for a model or hire someone well known to teach a specific technique. They were good years but I stopped after my hip surgery. Too hard to schlep all my stuff. The arrangement here [at the independent living facility] with the art room is good for me.

I can't begin to put into words the losses we experience here–not just to death, but people we know moving into Assisted Living, developing Alzheimer's, dementia and no longer knowing us. Not good. Your letter reminded me I did not get the Gawande[6] book yet and I ordered it, got a confirmation of my order right after you told me about it. I will track the order tomorrow.

I made a major decision and acted on it Friday. We have three buildings here and I live in the furthest from the main building which has the auditorium, dining room, library, and all the activity rooms. It is a very long walk from where I am and includes two open connecting corridors which are very cold. I love my view of the lake and pool and thought the walk would be good for me. It was. But now I am older and my balance is worse. Also, I am getting physical therapy once a week, so am up and back 2-3 times a day and that makes me too tired to do the exercises I need to do at home. I decided that maybe I should move into the main building. I saw the Executive Director and asked if there was anything available with a lake view that I could afford. She said she would check and to my surprise called me yesterday and told me to come look.

---

[6] Atol Gawande, *Being Mortal.*

Unbelievable–a newly redone apartment, slightly different layout than mine, with a view of the whole lake. Gorgeous and near the elevator. And she said because I give a lot to this community, it is affordable. Moving will be easy, practically no packing, everything on a dolly and wheeled over and maintenance will come and hang my paintings, connect TV, put up my dining room fixture. I am definitely looking into a Havanese [dog] and plan on January.

My daughter Bonnie is very funny–She loves the idea of the move because she thinks I will be healthier longer and save money on assisted living or an aide.

Two new book topics–dealing with loss in this kind of community and our children's attitudes/responses.

Love,

Myra

December 2, 2014

Dear Myra,

Are you there? Are you ok? Figured you'd be consumed (no pun intended) with Thanksgiving. I've been hurting much and probably looking at another hip operation.[7] Don't know anything definite yet but will see doc tomorrow and ought to have more specifics then. I'd like to get it done asap because I want to be there for [daughter] Alexa's play opening at Oregon Shakespeare Festival in March and for the Panama cruise with [son] Ben mid-April. Whenever it happens, my guess is it will be 2-3 weeks before we can get started again.

BUT: I've had some important ideas for our book about loss. Even invented a new developmental stage ala Erickson (his last was 65 on to death, and wrong, I think) When I hear from you, will try to write my thoughts.

Also, going to forward you a link about a Wall St. Journal article on aging.

Love, Max

December 2, 2014

I am here, Max–and OK. I had a feeling you were not feeling well and so sorry it is still hip trouble. You will probably hate this, but I am not surprised. Everyone I know who kept trying different things rather than get it done and over with has suffered. And I blame doctors for that. You

---

[7] MBJ: My left hip had been replaced about 2012. It kicked up an old dog injury which wouldn't go away and caused me a lot of intense pain. When the right hip was replaced in early 2015 it took away the pain completely and gave me a fluidity of movement I hadn't had in years.

have such good things to look forward to, so take care of yourself.

There is a very bright, lovely gentleman here with terrible scoliosis–can barely walk. Very independent and uses a scooter most of the time. The first night I went to dinner here, he rode over to me and asked if I would like to join him and two others for dinner. He is an avid reader and often gives me a book to read and then discuss it with him. He just gave me *How doctors think.* I told him I am reading [Gawande's] *Being mortal.* I will give it to him when I finish it. He will read it and then we will discuss both. I already think there are some very interesting comparisons.

I stayed in Florida for Thanksgiving and Karen and Marvin and I had dinner with my brother-in-law and his family in Miami. Good decision.

Incidentally, my decision to move is a *fait accompli.* I am in my new apartment. The kitchen is smaller, which is fine, given all the cooking I do (or don't do.) The dining and living room area is larger–lovely; the same patio and lake view–which I love. And, as I wanted, I have less walking to get to main areas. Bonnie and I will go to Bed, Bath and Beyond.

Please Max, take care of yourself and do it right this time. You are young enough to do well and not suffer like this. You and I are mortal, but we are gonna be as immortal as possible. Let me know how you are and what you are doing.

Love,

Myra

December 3, 2014

Dear Myra,

Great to hear from you. I think your move is a good decision. I read almost to the end of the Gawande book and at the end, I began to cry, so I stopped–probably about ten pages from the end. To stop if it got too sad, was a deal I made with myself. I loved the book and thought it very wise. Plan to give to my kids.

About hip: While I think you are right about docs (and they're all so fragmented and departmentalized these days) I HAVE done all the "right" things and that's what's been so frustrating. I had left hip replaced. That's fine now except for a creak now and then, which kicked up old soft tissue injury in the right side, which is what I've been struggling with–cortisone etc and thinking it would heal. It didn't. Now it looks like I need to have the right hip replaced, which may start the whole process of pain again. I sure hope not. Will keep you posted.

About loss: I have been thinking about your losses and your memorial services and etc. and feeling so sad for you about them. And this irony has come to me: If you put people in a place together–as we do–when they are 70-100 year olds, it is quite likely that there will be a lot of deaths. If we believe–as I do and as they say in therapy–that the process of saying goodbye stirs up goodbyes in the past, then people who live in those places are regularly experiencing new losses which stir up the old. Are they supposed to *practice*?

As I said before, Eric Erickson added another developmental stage to his protocol: age 65 on and called it "The Final Stage." It is integrity vs. despair. Erickson says when you get to this stage, you look back and if you feel good about your life you have "integrity," otherwise you "despair."

I think he's absolutely wrong. He seems to be in the "Life Review" box of some years ago and just looking back. I think we need at least another stage (and maybe a couple more.) It should be a stage not simply mired in the past, but also about the present and even the future. One stage I've called "Loss vs. Adaptation"–but that's just an idea. I was thinking that somehow I feel differently about loss at this age than I did before. Wadda you think?

Love,

Max

December 4, 2014

Hi Max,

I have been thinking–and I realize that what I think about and occasionally talk about with a very few other residents are challenges and adjustments as we age. In Erickson's time, people didn't live this long or even have time to retire. I think physical changes and loss represent challenges we must adjust to. I think if we can't acknowledge these "happenings," we ultimately lose ourselves.

Love,

Myra

December 4, 2014

Dear Myra,

If I remember correctly, Erickson first took his stage theory to about age 65. Then he got older and discovered "more" development and invented the last stage, 65 on (I think much was actually done by his wife.) I once saw him speak at UCLA in his later years. He was such a hero of mine, I wanted to see him before it was too late. I did a tiny drawing of him. He seemed pretty much out of it, but walked on the stage upright, as I recall. He died at 92 in 1994. I bet he had discovered a lot more life stages by then!

I agree with you about physical changes and loss representing a challenge to adjust to with the danger of losing the Self very real. But here's what I also think about: When I was younger, I wanted to SEE everything (e.g. if someone stuck me with a needle for a routine blood draw, I looked.) Now I have a list of things I don't want to "see" (like the Holocaust and slavery.) They are things I can't do anything about and to see the emotions and feel the emotions upsets me a great deal. For example, I'd love to be able to get everything working better in the Middle East but... It's probably about recognizing my all-too-real personal, cultural, national, global (and etc.) limitations. I believe that unplanned and unforeseen events are usually what cause change anyway–like what's going on now in Ferguson and NYC.[8]

I have wondered about the impact of "loss of looks," for women, as one grows older. The American culture is so youth oriented, specific and demanding about how a woman should look and, indeed, shaming if they don't look that way. I suspect this "loss" is more difficult than actual increasing body fragility and problems. I have a friend who was considered very beautiful and got a lot of attention for that. As she ages she has become "invisible" and she is having a terrible time.

I never thought myself pretty as a young girl. I was not the stereotypical, acceptable blue eyed wasp blond. And from an early age, about ten, I thought I weighed too much, which unfortunately is not atypical. The environment pounded me with this message. At best, I was called then "interesting looking." And that's what I was alright. But it simply didn't fit in. When I look back at the few photographs of me then, I was quite beautiful but in an "interesting" and unusual way. Few girls or women think of "unusual" as good. I sure didn't. Like most other women, I spent a

---

[8] And with our current presidential administration and North Korea!

lifetime trying to lose weight, filling my thoughts, mind and psychic space with worry and guilt and often feeling deprived. I lived in Los Angeles after all, which may have made it worse!

When I first came to Whidbey Island 16 years ago, when I was 65, I was invited to a birthday party. It was all women who spent the party time talking about their weight–usually it was too much–and their attempts at trying to solve their never-ending problem. I was shocked and determined to no longer give that issue time and space in my life or psyche. A few years ago when the image in the mirror began to look like my mother and some older person I didn't know, I decided to give up mirrors. I actually suggest this idea. The person I felt inside was full of energy and ideas and "young." The person I saw in the mirror was "old." How could I reconcile these two selves? I still have one mirror above my bathroom sink, to brush my teeth, comb my hair and put on my makeup–but that's all. I have no others and consciously resist checking my reflection in other places, like in the shower door. The result for me has been a resolution where I feel much younger (about 15, usually–only smarter) without a wrinkley image to constantly remind me that I'm not.

So what happens when, in a place like yours, a person comes up against so much loss? Do people live longer or "happier" if the loss (as in my life) is more distant and even less often? What might be the unconscious scheme here? If I get to it, maybe I'll write Gawande and see what he thinks.

I see the doc (specialist) for my hip in Seattle today. Originally, it was to be a second opinion about my soft tissue, ongoing pain. Now it's about hip replacement. Will keep you posted. Am supposed to bring shorts! HA. I wonder when was the last time that I owned shorts.

Love,

Max

December 4, 2014

Dear Max,

I do hope you get the right recommendation from the doc and can move on. I know how bad that pain can be.

As to Erickson: I remember he and his wife moved into a big house in Cambridge when they retired and surrounded themselves with college students. Somewhere I read that they wanted to be with young people.

We have raised some interesting questions and expressed some interesting thoughts that we need to include in our book. I had a spontaneous, impromptu, unsolicited interview with a resident today. She described her decision to move here as a new "adventure."

More important, let me know what is happening with you. And when you feel better, I will tell you how much we think alike regardless of our different circumstances.

Love,

Myra

December 7, 2014

Dear Myra,

Report: Saw the big honcho orthopedic surgeon in Seattle and, no surprise, I have to have a hip operation ("I don't know how you managed this long.") The scheduling may take it until January. Good news was he was completely agreed with Whidbey surgeon and knew him well. (I like the Whidbey guy very much, although probably to the right of the tea party politically.)

Once again, it means being in the hospital for a few days and then a recovery, because everything has to grow back. Last time, because I live alone, after the hospital I went for a week to a rehab facility. This time I hope Ben [son] will be able to take care of me at home. But, as to our work, it probably means my head won't work well for a few weeks because of pain meds etc. After I settle on when and where, then planning begins–care for my doggy etc.–uggg. Apparently, everybody saves their operations up until the end of the year because of insurance, vacations, which makes scheduling difficult. I just want to get the damned thing over so I have a hope of making my daughter's play opening and cruise with son. I am looking forward to the operation and to it making at least some difference, as I have been dealing with pretty intense pain for about two years now–as you well know. Drat!! FYI: I asked about the "minimally invasive operation" that is supposed to be quicker recovery, less pain. They said "marketing!"

As to our book together: I KNOW we think a lot alike–it is one reason I love you. I am keeping all our emails, back and forth, because at this point, I think they will be the major part of the book. Maybe our thoughts to each other over about a year. I know I don't want to do any formal interviews although I widely talk about the book and get ideas from everyone.

Here's something I learned this week: Washington is a "death with dignity"–assisted suicide state. The law went through in a recent election. I don't know the procedure, although I do know you have to get two docs attest to the fact you don't want to do it because of depression and then there is a "panel." An older person I know vaguely whose husband of many years died recently and was living in "Assisted Living," first called people to say goodbye, met with the panel and offed herself–neatly at the beginning of the month (so I guess nobody had to pay her rent for the month.) I don't know how she did it, but I thought it took guts (and apparently a prior agreement with her children.) No. I'm not planning that.

I am proofing a book for money. Arranged it way back in summer and although wouldn't do it now, I said I would, so I am. It's a more than 400-page manuscript and not the kind of book I would ordinarily read. My four Antioch [University] student mentees come tomorrow. They come out to Whidbey once a month. We talk, then we go to lunch.

Ben was awarded his Brazil grant, but NOT his grant on PREP. (PREP is a pill, FDA approved, few or no side effects, 100% effective, which keeps you from getting AIDS. For example, if you have a partner who has it, YOU don't get it.) I'm no conspiracy theorist, but I wonder about the politics of all this. PREP is largely unknown and quite controversial (some gays think it might change risk aversive behaviors for the worse.) I've talked to some doctors about it who never heard of it!

All for now,

Love,

Max

December 7, 2014

Dear Max,

No surprise about your hip operation. I think we both knew this was where you were headed. I'm glad you will be fine after all of this.

I am out of the creative box too, for at least two weeks until I am settled enough in my new apartment to start making notes. I have been printing off our "significant" correspondence and have it in a folder.

Just let me know when you go in for surgery and where you are.

Love,

Myra

January 3, 2015

Dear Myra,

I don't know if you got Harriet's christmas letter and wanted to share it with you. I think it is very apropos of our book.

Love,

Max

Harriet Wadeson's[9] Christmas Letter

December 2014

Dear Friends,

Apologies for no holiday letter last year. In Oct. 2013 after I had returned from Ohio where I had been a conference keynote speaker, workshop leader and teacher of a full-day course, I came down with chills, so much so

---

[9] Harriet Wadeson died January 26, 2016 at the age of 85. She was a good friend to Max and Myra. Harriet was a pioneering art therapist for over 50 years entered the field in the 1960s through her work at the National Institutes of Health in Washington, D.C. She was the author of eight books, founder and director of art therapy training programs at the University of Houston, University of Illinois at Chicago and Northwestern. She was the author of the no-holds-barred *Journaling cancer in words and images* (2011, Charles C Thomas, publisher.) which many consider a masterpiece of its kind. No "cancer is a gift" kind of book, it is a hard-hitting story that tells what it is really like to have cancer and go through cancer treatment.

that my teeth were chattering. Several doctor visits later, I was diagnosed with acute leukemia. It was a good thing it didn't happen before I went to Ohio, because the conference had been planned for a year, so I was glad I didn't leave them high and dry. (But my days doing those engagements may be over.) I was started on chemo, hospitalized and then sent to the skilled nursing unit here at The Mather [Assisted Living Community] for six weeks. I was sick for most of the winter (the coldest in forever) before I returned to my apartment. I have continued the chemo and feel fine most of the time. I am on a 28 day-cycle with chemo on the first seven days, shots instead of drips and not as toxic as the chemo I had for the uterine cancer five years ago. (I've been discharged by the oncologist as being "cured" from that.)

Though I still feel too vulnerable to travel, we did go to Door County in the summer and briefly in the spring and fall, although on one occasion, I passed out in a tai chi class had had to be driven in an ambulance to the hospital an hour away.

But mostly I am fine. At the moment, I am immersed in writing the Mather Holiday Play, which is a send-up of the Mather, called "the Blather" in the play. I've written some songs for it too, and we'll even have some dancing. I'll play Mrs. Claus, which should be great fun.

This place is full of contradictions. So many enjoyable things to do and nice people to do them with. (Currently I have an art show up of paintings of Door County that I painted there.) And yet so many here have had one illness or another. And, of course, some friends have died. N fell and hit her head so now she is in skilled nursing. Fortunately, she continues to improve and is now walking with a walker. So this month, I have been spending much of my time visiting her there. We both realize that it is a good thing we moved to The Mather to deal with all that has befallen us. But seeing the patients in skilled nursing, many of whom are there permanently, can be depressing.

...So how do I feel about having leukemia? Mainly I would say that I am the Queen of de-Nile and live from day to day. It is impossible for me to imagine myself dead. I continue to be grateful for all the beauty of this world and wish we weren't messing it up. I appreciate those who love me and those who are kind to me, and the many pleasant memories I have with them.

I hope this holiday seasons finds you well and happy and that the New Year will bring you all your heart desires.

I have hopes too for all those who suffer war, hunger and disease with the wish that their suffering will abate and the gratitude that we are living so much more privileged lives.

With love,
Harriet

PART II

2015

March 19, 2015

(This letter concerns "The Myra Levick Award for Excellence in Art Therapy" that Myra and I were working on. To date it has been awarded to four people, including Harriet Wadeson. It arose from our joint conviction that the American Art Therapy Association was not awarding its highest honor to some (older) art therapists who had contributed a great deal to the profession. Myra was designing a certificate and struggling with her computer.)

Dear Max,

This award certificate IS centered. However, I lost the gold color–who knows why? Computers!

Remember, the first page is blank, it is printed horizontally and the parchment paper (it is printed on) is textured and makes a difference.

I am done until Sunday. I am doing my taxes.

Love,

Myra

March 20, 2015

Dear Myra,

I liked the first award certificate better–but I understand the computer difficulties and I think YOU should decide.

Re your story about your facility and computers: A number of years ago, [Son] Ben got tired of my computer questions to him and for Xmas gave me a gift certificate to a computer class at South Whidbey High School. I went and there were about six people in the class. They were all, kind of like me—older and wanting to know the basics, like where the on/off switch was. I discovered a major problem was that the teacher was a computer "expert" and in no way could think as simplistically as we needed (she was a young person). So I found it useless and continued to ask Ben questions. He is my computer "consultant" and after I have struggled with a computer problem for an hour, I call him where ever he is in the world. I think he has given up trying to *teach me* how to do it and is resigned to simply telling me *how*. That's what I want.

I used to go to a painting class at the Senior Center and there was an older lady who taught computers–and the room was always filled—about 30 people (I would go past it on the way to the bathroom). So a lot of people are wanting to learn, I'd say.

One of the great difficulties for you, my dear, is that your mind is as tight as a drum! And I think that is unusual for someone your age—or is that a stereotype? Your writings recently make me wonder if "Assisted Living" (when I say that, I mean ALL the levels) enhances passivity and perhaps the loss of one's marbles. "Independent Living" seems like an oxymoron. Wadda you think? I imagine that being "with it" is maybe a disadvantage in your sort of environment. Or is it the rather passive "culture" that has been prevalent for women and therefore just a continuation? Ben, when he was here, read Gawande's book. He got to the last 30 pages and asked me "What does he say the ANSWER is?" I said, he doesn't say and doesn't know—raising the questions at this point is what seems important.

Love,

Max

December 22, 2015

Dearest Myra,

Let me know what you think about the following and if you want to go forward! First: I liked your intro and will write an accompanying piece (from me) to go with it. (And will send to you)

Some of the words you used, which are fine for an intro, made me realize that I want to be clear about my intentions for our book. (Much of this I have said along the way, but I think it is worth saying again, here.)

The words from your intro problematic for me are "challenge" and "adventure." I consider both of these jargon—and, again, while they are fine for an intro, hewing to them within the rest of the book is NOT the kind of book I want to write—e.g. "Challenge" is what they use these days for "problems." It is supposed to be less negative. What it IS for me is quite general, intentionally neutral and eliminates the possibility that there *are* plenty of cultural impediments which are intractable problems, not simply "obstacles" to get around. I think the word "challenges" might enhance guilt. No problem though, if you want to continue to use the word "challenge."

Why I want to do the book with YOU? Because we are both smart, thoughtful, insightful, write fairly well and have something to say about "aging" and our experiences of it that hasn't been said before and I think that is worth doing. What we are usually is specific and detailed.

From what I have seen in my "research" on the literature of aging, most writing is "funny" or making fun of aging or saying, humorously, the usual stereotypes are not true. The "old age is not for sissies" kind of thing. What very little "real" research there is has reported on aging people (their population) *in facilities* of one kind or another and therefore reports on that group as if it were the norm or representative of all. It reminds me of way back in the 1970s when I was doing a thesis for social work school and looking for literature on secular and orthodox Jewish women. There was plenty of literature and research on orthodox and virtually none on secular, because, obviously the orthodox could be easily found (synagogues, Jewish neighborhoods etc.) and secular could not because they were dispersed into the rest of the American population.

While I expect our book will have humor in it, I do not want to write a humor book. I see ours as a different kind of book because of who we both are. I want our book to be about our own experiences and thoughts.

Method? Over time we have been talking about this and we have been through some different formats, from a research project on. I believe we have settled on an email dialogue which I discovered is called an "epistolary" book.

Obviously, it was letters and documents before, not emails. Title: *Dear Myra, Dear Max*. This way we can write about our daily lives, our thoughts, a topic or two if we want to–like health or humor or kids. I propose that we make a commitment to write about one time a week to each other, keep them in Dropbox and see where we are after six months.

I think it's necessary for us to be on the same page before going forward–???

Much love,

Max

December 22, 2015

Dear Max,

We must be on the same page, and we are. I did not want to make the intro too heavy for fear it might scare people away.

For me, challenge leads to problems and adventure leads to solutions and hopefully, adjustments. That is the process living here [in an Independent Living facility] and I will try to put these thoughts into a letter. I also want to interview some individuals and couples and see if the process is the same or different for them. And how does all that relate to someone in your position, living alone?

What I did not put into the intro [prologue] is that I was also inspired by Gawande whose major thesis is *respect* for the aged. Many are quite capable of thinking for themselves and making independent decisions, even though they are sometimes treated like children. If I can bypass Gawande's medical perspective, I will try to weave some of that in.

And yes, [daughter] Marsha's title is funny, but I certainly never thought of using it. Seriously, loss of hearing, especially living with a group of people is another not funny problem. I liked most of the chapter titles/topics you listed in one letter. To start writing, I thought of going over that and addressing what strikes a chord with me.

Max, What I really want this book to be is to make my cohorts aware that we can control some things, but must accept those we can't; I want to make "management" aware of how difficult this might be for some and pay more attention to "us" than to landscaping gardens and courtyards.

And to you I can say many people here look to me as a "role model" because I am always, well dressed, friendly and involved. They should only know. To you I can express my frustration.

My challenge/problem is to say all this so it goes down easy enough and I do think we can do it because, if you are getting old, no matter where or how you live, in the end, you are in charge of yourself.

Are we on the same pages?

Love,

Myra

December 23, 2015

Dear Myra,

Yes, we are on the same page! And 1 am certainly prepared to go on and "get going."

I want to respond to a couple of things you said, like about not expressing anger, frustration etc. While it may be necessary in the real world and in an independent living facility and the like to be "culturally acceptable," I strongly urge us to not filter things and not to try to "make it go down easy." I think the point of our book is to have *everything* that two smart 'aging' women are feeling and saying. I know ours are probably universal stories. Hopefully, we will go deep and be more thoughtful. I think the more "Negative" emotions are part of being human.

I think it is particularly important for us to not filter and to express what we feel, for many reasons, but for none more than that women of our era (and most eras) are trained to be "Good Girls." While they often feel most of it, they have managed to stamp it out, because it is not kosher to express "negative" feelings or have a "conflict" or God forbid a "confrontation." (I know a therapist here who has a practice full of seriously conflicted couples—he loves it because he says there's lots of good, strong stuff to work with! Lots of "confrontation.")

Through our eyes, our hearts and our intensity, I know others will relate because it will resonate with them, even if many can't express what they feel. There's a topic right there: The need to be "acceptable." As one who is known as "direct"–not always meant as a complement, I would imagine living in a facility one needs to try to be "acceptable."

No. Loss of hearing is not a funny problem. Somebody said to me recently that having eye troubles, people give you sympathy because they can SEE the symptoms, but hearing problems usually can't be seen and can be very very isolating and I think that's quite profound. I wonder if the problem of denial by the hearing impaired is greater too because of that. I have a friend here who doesn't hear well. We go to the movies together and, at the Clyde Theater, one can get free ear phones which feed you the dialogue. She regularly forgets to pick them up.

Remember I grew up with a deaf mother who worked hard to appear "normal," and did a lot of counseling of people sent to her by the ear docs to help them adjust to wearing hearing aids which were then very visible. I wonder if, ironically, "unseeable" hearing aids are actually such an advantage—whereas my mother, at the beginning wore a 5-lb battery pack on her leg, and a huge hearing aid pinned to her blouse with visible wires going to the ear buds. I think they were even black wires. Another instance of does our amazing technology make things better or simply more invisible and therefore more "normal"?

I'm going to send this to you, and then put both our replies in "Dropbox" as I think this is worthwhile to us, as our dialogue about defining our book.

Onwards and upwards!

Max

PART III

2016

January 19, 2016

Dear Max,

I'm having my melanoma surgery Thursday morning and wanted to do as much writing as I could before. I am attaching what I have written so far and hopefully will finish this piece tomorrow evening. Tonight at dinner, I got the five women I eat with to tell me why they came to this place. And I have notes to add on along with a few more I want to collect on this topic. I always print what I write and look forward to your comments, or the next chapter.

Love,

Myra

January 24, 2016

Dear Myra,

First, I was thinking about the melanoma on your face and your "scar." While I am so sorry that you had to go through it at all, it seems to me that maybe now you will wear on your face what has been inside. Having known you for a lot of years, I consider you (and this is a complement) a street fighter in all the best ways. One thing I like best is your relentless anger and high expectations. As women of this American culture, we are still expected to "look our best," not to mention the old saw of "not letting yourself go." Even though older people, particularly women, become invisible, we have internalized that view and usually try to make the effort. I realized a long time ago that I could wear my underwear on the outside of my clothes to an event and if anyone noticed at all, they would just say "she's eccentric!"

As you were looking at potential homes for you after Len's death, I thought the question "What do you want?" was so poignant, so right on, and unfortunately so seldom asked. I loved that you noticed it and noticed its omission in other facilities you looked at. A few years back, when I thought I would have to sell my house because I was running out of money to live on, I looked into a few "Retirement Homes." I looked at the one here on south Whidbey and a few others in Seattle and the "mainland" including one non-profit and one for retired academics– presumably heavy on intellectual pursuits. Judging from websites and information brochures, they were all about the same. They showed professional photos of happy-looking seniors, usually a heterosexual couple, sometimes an older woman, listed the different levels of living facilities they offer, focused on transportation (particularly to doctors) and on the multitude of activities offered. Most were mid-sized; some were huge with hundreds of inhabitants. All were expensive. I would have had to sell my house to have even a beginning of enough money.

As pretty much an introvert at this time of my life, I like my separateness–my writing and painting, and I don't play bridge. I want my interactions with people to have the potential to be meaningful. I grew up in a time and in a family where *conversation* was a pleasurable activity and now live in a world where deep, expanding and far-reaching conversation has all but disappeared. I value authenticity and have little interest in "small" talk, although I understand it as a form of social connection. I have spent a lifetime trying *not* to tell the truth when the market cashier asks "How are you?" I think my time is the most valuable thing I have and I don't want to waste it.

Although I like the things around me that have meaning to me–paintings, books, photographs and especially my folk art, living in a smaller space would not be a problem for me; I live a lot in my head anyway, and always have. I thought the "Retirement community" format was not for me, as of now, anyway. There are too many rules and there was the unwritten assumption that many,

many activities were a good thing. (In fact, one facility I inquired about, called me the following week to ask me to teach art.)

I have been living alone for a long time and even though there are sometimes difficult tradeoffs to that, I like it. (I support singer James Taylor's statement: "You have to have some loneliness to have freedom.") I am long divorced and my grown children live their own lives in Los Angeles and New York. To be fair, perhaps if I had looked longer and deeper at retirement facilities, I might have seen the possibility for more individual differences, but as it was, I saw a kind of well-intentioned "crowd mentality." I even tried to talk about how a person would be viewed if an, I can't resist the term, "inmate," tended to not participate in activities, but they, understandably, didn't know what I was talking about.[10]

Atol Gawande's viewpoint in his *Being Mortal* is that most seniors placed in retirement facilities are to assuage the children, because, quite naturally, they want their older parents to be safe. Safety is obviously an issue as one ages,

---

[10] Research shows that seniors who have friends and social interactions do better. As my (MBJ) friend, the doctor, says "They didn't ask introverts!"

but I believe that the multiple needs and wishes of older people cannot be generalized nor lumped into one bag.

That question, "What do you want?" is necessary. And asking that question of the people who are the "consumers" seems smart and crucial. I wonder why it's typically not done. Physical caretaking is one thing. Is this another assumption or myth that older people no longer have emotional needs or desires? Plain old safe caretaking is not enough for most people. The over 75 crowd are social pioneers that we haven't looked at yet. Looking away and putting them in "places" where they are safe reminds me of what they used to do with the mentally ill in "asylums." That is, a problem that cannot be solved should be humanely as out of sight as possible.

I look forward to hearing from you!

Love,

Max

March 13, 2016

Dear Myra,

I have read over again your letter about looking for an "independent" living place. I especially liked all the specifics and think they will be very helpful to those who may undertake the same journey. I loved, although I wasn't surprised from YOU, your insistence on doing it YOUR way—it's a good model! So many "elders" simply are passive in their approach to this, using the facility or perhaps their children, as the "authority" and going along with what is suggested. I believe *knowing what you want and being willing to try get it* is an important trait at any age. This is especially difficult for women, of course, who are brought up to be passive caretakers and to "go along with the plan." Somehow as one ages and is supposed to "deteriorate," the fact of being active on your own behalf–if you ever were– as it is mandated by the culture, is supposed to somehow disappear and go away. All too often, one is left (easier that way for all, I guess) as a dependent moosh, who is supposed to go along with just about anything and especially not make trouble. Nobody likes a complainer, after all. The trade-off is you get taken care of and your children are happy.

My father used to say that "the older you get, the more like yourself you become." (He also said, "It's important to make the right enemies.") A person like you who has lived an active life, confidently following her own path, is not likely to change–nor should have to–as she grows older. That we sit around and "deteriorate" is one of those myths. I understand that retirement "facilities" have different levels of independence and care, and I understand that one's body does stop spinning along as it may have once done, but even with the best of intentions and some geriatric knowledge, what is provided in institutions for "seniors" tends to be a generic, bureaucratic system of rules. From what I know, people, to that point, who have been quite fine at charting their own individualistic path, are then expected to "fit in." And not doing that, has ramifications. Doing what one needs to do to be "happy" is hardly an issue that should be a problem. I certainly understand that most administrators, caretakers etc. are well intentioned and that it may be impossible to run a facility on an individualistic basis, but for somebody with an active brain, used to doing her own thing and making her own rules, it must be like requiring a lobotomy at times.

I worked this quarter with a very bright art therapy student who had a practicum in a retirement home. (A practicum, in her program is pre-internship and just one quarter.) Although she was not there long, she was there long enough and is smart enough to understand the system.

When she left, and said goodbye, of course it stirred up stuff in the people she had seen and in herself. She was lucky to have me to talk to and to understand the quite obvious dynamics of loss evoked. But as far as I could tell, this was not an issue in the practicum site (nor in her grad program) and that people come and go in the retirement home is neither noticed nor attended to. Do you think that there is so much coming and going at that life stage that ignoring it is the best that people can do? I know, at least at your facility, there are sometimes memorial services etc.

Personally, I feel somewhat differently about death than I did at a younger age. Obviously, the older one gets, the more likely it is to happen–to oneself or to people we care about. I believe living a life (well) is learning to let go– e.g. we practice on our kids, who grow up, leave and construct their own lives whether we like them or not: And that's actually what we want them to do.

The people I love who have died, somehow now I seem more able to let go of them and not feel the huge wound of loss I might have once felt–e.g. my Dad died over 40 years ago, but I still remember him constantly (and have quoted him here.) When my Dad died at age 64, from my vantage point at age 30, I thought he had lived a long and good life. Now, at 78 and a half, I think he was quite young! The going on, of course, is necessary and healthy–I wonder if you would be willing to talk about how you manage/d Len's death?

Thanks for recognizing my exhaustion about finishing the "Con Safos" book, my 9th, I am tired, but I'll get over that. This a.m. I went to the post office when it opened to send the manuscript to Jess Trevino in Los Angeles so he can write the Foreword. Yes, it was/is a labor of love–it has many meanings. One is that it will be the first documentation of a very important event of Chicano history. Another, to me, is that it continues the thread of my personal social justice quest and activities.

I wouldn't have taken it on if I weren't interested and curious and I learned a great deal and had fun–until about 2/3rds of the way through, when I got bored. (My friends tell me that's when I start referring to it as "that stupid book.") Boredom or not, it was important for me to finish and thus the struggle. I thought about my own stuff–was my finishing or not finishing about my own issues of looming mortality? And decided it was not. I simply like to finish what I start–always have. (On the Meyers Briggs Personality Inventory, for better or worse, I am a "J"–for "judgment." A "J" is not about judging but is someone who likes closure. The opposite type is "P" for "perceiving"–

many starts, few finishes. "J"s are the people who organize and are more rare.)

Before my hip operation, when I was hurting so and was quite depressed from the years of pretty intense pain, there was little I wanted to live for–except I wanted to finish this book. Now I will pick up the stuff that has been left hanging and take it easy for a while. I wrote the book partially for my "Con Safos" friends and knew I could get finished–they are probably all "P"s. But I also wrote it for me–not for the money, but to get their story out into the world.

And speaking of "picking up," I will end this letter here and go and do a few other things. Then I plan to lie on the bed, watch "Judge Judy"–if the wretched March Madness basketball doesn't pre-empt it, and perhaps take a delicious nap.

Much love,

Max

March 14, 2016

Oy Vey, Max,

About computers: Very few people outside of staff know how to use computers and very few have them. There are two old computers in the library and hardly anyone uses them. Would you believe that beside the financial office, Executive Director, and the Activities Director I am probably the most literate computer person here? I make all the flyers for anything I am involved in and the Activity director makes most for the others. Now she is checking with me to be more creative with graphics. No matter how you slice it, the folks here are old folks–a generation of women who for the most part did not work and men who ran businesses. We did have someone in human services who could and would help with computer problems if I needed him, but he is long gone. One maintenance man here is great at connecting the computer and printer, but I can do that if I don't have to get on the floor. And I am lucky to have one son-in-law who is fabulous at photoshop and the other loves email. My daughters are not as savvy as I am and do not use the photoshop programs I use.

The good news is that I (usually) really like the challenge to do something new. I just get so frustrated when

I want to do something NOW and can't get it right. So tonight I am doing spread sheets to check in the women for the monthly Ladies Luncheon tomorrow. Boring, but no sweat.

Love,

Myra

March 15, 2016

Dear Myra,

Your computer tales are interesting, and unfortunately not surprising. Oy vey is right! I was thinking about an idea to help and came up with the facility paying an IT guy a bit, so people from your place could call with questions. It seems to me it would be a good marketing tool for Assisted Living places. That's a real generational gap, isn't it? I think I'll ask Harriet[11] what the computer situation is at her Assisted Living place, The Mather.

Did you happen to see "Citizen Four" about Edward Snowden? About the first half was all about computers and in a language I didn't speak—if they'd kept that up, I would have quit watching--but they didn't. The movie made me

---

[11] MBJ: I did not know that Harriet had already died in January.

realize how there's this whole world out there in computer-land that lots know about, lots!

Love,

Max

April 6, 2016

Dear Max,

Your letters in March touched on so many of the issues and dynamics I am confronted with daily, I have been struggling with where to begin. It has been like standing in front of a blank canvas and deciding if I am going to just start painting and see what happens, or draw in a structure to contain my flight of ideas. I have chosen a middle road, follow your letter and respond as your words evoke images of my life before here and now.

Going after what I wanted is a trait I first remember exercising in my teens. I lived in a community that made it possible for me to choose one of two high schools. One was considered one of the best in the city. The other was rated lower–partly, I now believe, because the population was so diverse. As I approached graduation from Junior High I learned this school was going to include art as a fifth major in the academic track—the first in the city. I told my parents that was where I wanted to go. I was lucky. I was a good student and they had assumed I would automatically go to the better school, but knowing my love of art, reluctantly they supported my decision. Going to that school proved to be a wise choice and informed some of my future choices. At sixteen, I made another significant choice: I told my parents I was "going steady" with my childhood sweetheart and would not date anyone else. This time they tried to discourage me, but finally gave up, accepting the fact that we planned to marry when we were old enough. As you know, this was the most important and the very best decision I ever made.

Your memories of your father's wise words (which I will come back to because they are so relevant to aging) reminded me of two things my father told me in those early years. The first was in reference to my decision at sixteen: Len (my future husband) was a pre-med student and from the time he was a teen ager knew he wanted to be a doctor. Surprisingly (given their cultural heritage) my parents were not impressed that I would be a "doctor's wife." My father told me this was not going to be an easy life and I should be prepared. He also told me then, and many times over the years, don't do anything you don't want to and then whine about it. He was right about the first and made me always alert to the second throughout my life. All relevant to my aging and to who and where I am today–and to my peers in this community.

Coincidentally, I visited a neighbor yesterday, as I had promised her several weeks ago. She celebrated her 100th birthday a few months back and doesn't join us for dinner as frequently as she used to do. Mentally, she is as sharp as she has ever been–and will tell you so. I agree that it is a myth that as we age we "sit around and deteriorate." I do believe some people do just that but for a variety of reasons, but the process cannot be generalized. Here, I bring my friend, (who I shall call Eve,) into our correspondence because she asked me a very interesting question: "When I look around here, what do I see?" Frankly, I was not sure what she was asking and she explained, when she looks around she sees lots of "has beens"–people who may have been active, productive, involved in the past; now just sitting around and fulfilling the myth of "deteriorating." Interesting. I see the very opposite: people who are "wanna bes"; people who didn't do some of the things they wanted to and now feel free to explore new connections, new activities, new challenges in our so called "independent living" community.

Eve and I are both right. It doesn't take long to realize, not only are we dependent on a set of rules and schedules, but "fitting in" is paramount to moving forward. My friend Eve is a perfect example of my perspective. This facility was originally a hotel. Around 25 years ago, seeing the handwriting on the wall, management converted the rooms to retirement apartments. Eve, then in her mid 80s, was among the first to move in. Widowed twice, she raised three children and had been living independently in her own home is South Florida for 16 years. Very gregarious and outgoing, she became friends with an interesting couple here–the husband, (a retired professor) and his wife, an editor and proof reader for publications written by her husband and her father before him. I will call her Joan. Within a few years after settling here, the husband became ill and passed away. Using her skills, Joan designed, edited and printed a journal three times a year called "The Round Table." She invited a few resident writers, former writers and wanna-be writers to contribute. She encouraged people who had interesting stories to write them and she would edit and include them in an issue. Her journal became the voice of the residents in this community.

I mention Joan because Eve told me that this remarkable lady, over ninety when I met her almost five years ago, helped her find a part of herself she never knew existed. Eve became an accomplished poet. For every issue of the journal there is at least one new poem by Eve, and sometimes two. In our recent meeting she gave me a bound collection of many of her lovely poems and at some point in our collaboration, I will share at least one or two. I consider neither of these women "has beens" or "wanna bes." They are incredible examples of mastering all the challenges of aging, adjusting to a new, sometimes restricting environment and "fitting in."

Joan gave up "The Round Table" at the end of this past year but continued to serve on the Residents Council and volunteered to organize and conduct a story reading activity. She passed away suddenly just four weeks ago and that loss and your letter about your student's experience evoked many thoughts and memories of personal and peer losses.

We have a tradition here that I sometimes think is when a lobotomy might have been a good idea. When someone dies, a vase of white roses, with a picture of the deceased, name and date, is placed on a credenza in the Lobby. Sometimes there is more than one and one week there were five. There is no way to avoid these beautiful, sad notices of death. To get information from the front desk, to get transportation, leave a maintenance request, check the weekly calendar of activities and events (including memorial services) we must go through the Lobby and pass these strategically placed ominous visions. I don't know of anyone who doesn't check them when they are there. For me, I sigh with relief if it is someone who has been in Assisted Living and not one of my cohorts in Independent living. To answer your question: it is almost impossible to ignore the loss of someone here, unless of course you are totally oblivious to your surroundings. And yes, there are memorial services, of all denominations, complete with a lovely food service prepared by the dining room manager. In the years I have been here, I have observed there are those who go to every memorial service, to pay their respects; there are those that go for the food they know will be served, regardless of how well they knew the deceased. But for me and others like me, it is depressing while at the same time providing closure on a relationship we enjoyed. It is also a time to offer condolences to family we have met or are just meeting. For Joan, there was no memorial service and some of us felt that as an additional loss. One of our mutual friends asked the Executive Director if a few of us could plan a memorial service for her but was told the family did not hold memorial services and she could not go against their wishes.

I would like to share one other unusual response simply to illustrate that sometimes, even in this generic community we meet someone who doesn't fit the mold. Before I came for my interview here, I was told, by a friend, to call someone she knew here and get her opinion. I did and after I moved in we were neighbors and became bridge partners and friends. I will call her Liddy. In spite of the fact that she was in her 70s, we had much in common. I learned she was here because she suffered from severe diabetes, had been widowed for over 20 years and needed this supportive community. But she was tough and had alienated as many men and women along the way as she had come to be close with. She really did not fit in. A year before she passed away, she befriended a new resident, taking her shopping, arranging bridge games for her and more. Within two months she shut Rose (as I will call her) out of all bridge games and attempted to exclude her from the Women's luncheon. Fortunately, I was able to prevent this. Within that year Rose made many other friends, found bridge partners and settled in; she fit in. After Liddy's death her family got together and planned a lovely memorial here. The point of this vignette is that Rose then approached me and asked if there was a specific charity to make a contribution to in Liddy's memory. Given their history I was surprised that she wanted to. I told her the family's preference and asked if she was going to the memorial service. She answered "no." She said Liddy was not her friend and going to her memorial was, in her mind, hypocritical. Making a contribution to the memory of someone in our community who has passed away, was a tradition in her religion and held no malice toward anyone. I thought about this and decided here was a very senior person with principles who continued to treat people like she would want them to treat her- whether they treated her that way or not: A "mensch."

Lastly, dear friend. You asked If I would be willing to talk about how I managed Len's death–and yes, I am willing to talk about it. But, Max, I don't think I managed his death; I survived it!

Four years ago, this past August, my 87th birthday was a week away and Len would have been 90 November first of that year. We were still going out to dinner, playing bridge with friends, at least once a week, going to the movies and literally sharing light housekeeping and laundry in our very comfortable two-bedroom apartment. I had started using a cane that past year due to recent hip surgery; Len had stopped playing tennis a few years before. We were walking slower but we were both still driving. While we were in generally good health I had asked him if he thought we should begin to consider an independent living community and this time, he said "absolutely not." He told me he just wanted to sit on the sofa with me and hold my hand while we watched TV. After almost 68 years of marriage, who could ask for anything more– especially since he promised to let go when I wanted to knit. One evening, that week, as we prepared for bed he told me he was more tired than usual and that kind of tired was not good. He said there was no need to call a doctor, or see one and I did what is typical for me, I shut off any concerns. Looking back, I now know, he was preparing me. Two nights later, shortly after falling asleep, he woke up suddenly, told me he was having trouble breathing and to call 911. Following the ambulance to the hospital. I was calm and told myself they would give him a pacemaker and we would be fine. My housewife/doctor education was correct (this time) and that was the decision. We were told he would be in cardiac ICU to be stabilized and surgery would probably be in 4-5 days. Len was admitted and I informed the nurses I would sleep there. One promptly began to berate me and said in no uncertain terms "this was not allowed." I told her there was a first time for everything and while she was getting angrier and redder, the other nurse walked out, came back with a pillow and blanket and led me to a little couch in their lounge. Len was "hooked up" and had a temporary pacemaker inserted and was initially very angry at the goings-on. During those four days we probably broke every visiting rule there was. Our three daughters and two sons-in-law, two grandsons and Len's brother and his wife all arrived the next day, came and stayed every day until the day of surgery. No one threw us out. The machines registered he was in good shape, and he seemed to enjoy the funny stories about being a big brother and a father of three daughters. I slept there every night and one of our daughters came every morning so I could go home, shower and change. Sunday the permanent pacemaker was installed. I was told everything was fine and the "machines" all registered perfect. The nurses, my good friends by then, told me to go home and get a good night's rest. He would be discharged the next day. I did and at 6AM the phone rang. It was the night nurse, crying as she told me Len had had a massive coronary and asking could they resuscitate him? His living will was very clear and my answer had to be no. It was August 24, 2011, 4 days after my 87th birthday.

Max, I learned many years ago that in a crisis, I go into, what I call my robot mode. I am fully aware of what has happened–there is no denying it–but literally, I put all feelings aside and do whatever I have to. I drove to the hospital, made the necessary arrangements there, met with my children to plan the service –a military one for the next day, according to Jewish law, and planned where and for how long we would sit "shiva." There was one thing I could not do – and that was to even imagine what I would say. While my daughters and brother in-law prepared their speeches, I decided I would speak for Len. I would read his ethical will which I had found in our file when I retrieved his living will. He had written it in 1976 and it was beautiful. No one asked me to do more.

I was surprised that my daughters did not want a memorial service. They wanted a party to celebrate his life on November 1, which would have been Len's 90th birthday. During the days of "shiva," we planned the party like one he would have loved to attend. A menu of his favorite home cooked meals and lots and lots of chocolate. And we invited only people we knew he would want there.

During those days, I also said no thank you to my children's invitations to live with them, made my decision to sell my apartment and move to a retirement community. The following month, I immersed myself in this project and signed a lease in mid-October. I still had to face the "empty spaces" in my apartment for the months of September and October, so I planned another project. I made a memory book of the service we held for Len. Far from denying my loss, I created a memorial that included a letter from me, Len's ethical will, our children's words and his brother's words. I also included a few special pictures, a poem the Rabbi read and a beautiful poem a colleague wrote on hearing of his death. I made one for me and for each of our daughters, grandchildren and Len's brother. It was my Chanukkah gift to all that year and the most healing experience I had.

I moved the week after the party and began to manage my new life.

Over the years, Max, you have said little about your divorce and how it impacted your current living style. Can you share that now?

Love,

Myra

May 19, 2016

Dear Myra,

Finally!! I have been finishing, reworking the *Con Safos* book [*Voices from the Barrio*] and trying to understand and line up a person to help me with on-demand publishing since I am a technological ninny and unwilling to spend the time necessary to technologically bring myself up to date in any way. E.g. what I know already serves me well enough and enables me to do what I want to do. (I have published eight books, after all!) I have no doubt I have the brain, still, to master the more advanced gadgets and processes although I could never achieve the status of "nerd" I simply don't want to spend the time–you know I am very protective of my time and try to use it as I want. There are couple of women I know that spend a lot of time with their gadgets. Then they spend a lot of time getting them sorted out, fixed, virus free and etc and talking to repair persons. Just realized they are not bridge players. Is the tech obsession at least for some older women, an individualized contemporary form of playing bridge? Or the way "retired" people fill up time?

You know, I am all for people doing what they want to as much as possible and that I think this is a particularly difficult task for women, and for women of our generations (and class, and probably race and ethnicity, to some extent) who are rewarded all their lives for caretaking, being a partner and relating as part of a pair and going along. They are generally not experienced in making their own decisions. Of course, one CAN be part of a pair, and still make your own decisions, but it is certainly more complicated and the culture is not "approving"–look at poor Hilary. And even Megan Kelly, the Fox News anchorwoman who had the famous encounter with Trump over his treatment of women. She said that in the same debate that night some of her male colleagues also hit Trump with hard, uncomfortable questions, but he never had the on-going nasty feud with them that he had with her.

I believe you and I are of the few women who have always driven their own course and we were lucky enough to have parents who went along with and even supported our choices. (I wonder if we would have listened had they not?) For example, your decision at age 16 to marry Len. At age 20, when I was going around Europe on a motorcycle with my boyfriend, I sent my parents some photos of me with my helmet on. They didn't mind that I was "living in sin." But they minded that I was going on a motorcycle, helmet or not and they expressed their dislike openly. Did I stop? No. I simply said "Then I won't tell you." (I did anyway and they got used to it, or at least stopped saying anything.)

I have always thought that you and the other women who formed the profession of art therapy and established the American Art Therapy Association (AATA) in the late 1960s were probably like that. They were working women with good brains, when women didn't work unless they had to. They were talented and aggressive. They had ideas, were difficult and were not afraid of argument. They were often married and I have always wondered if AATA gave them a place to be openly opinionated and argumentative when the "outside world" and possibly their marriages didn't.

Whether they were conscious of it or not, did AATA provide a needed structure for those talented women when the repressive culture did not? I always thought so.

Apropos of this and of valuing my time: There is a new program getting organized in my area, "Aging in Place." It has been a program in cities and towns nationally for a long time, but now someone I like and respect is getting it going here. I volunteered to be, I think they are calling them "Call Managers." This is the person on the other end of the line organizing services for those who call. I was prepared to volunteer my time to do this for a day a week and figured I'd had a lot of experience and could be useful. Here's what happened: First thing was I received an email saying that "Call Managers" would be using a new software system but that it was very user friendly and we would receive training soon. I figured that my dislike of "new software systems" was generational and maybe personal but I had doubts and emailed the man in charge. He suggested I could be an "Ambassador" instead–when someone wants to become a member, Ambassadors go out and talk to them. I told him I didn't want to be an Ambassador. I questioned him whether others were complaining about the need to learn new software. While he didn't consider I was "complaining, " he said, he had heard from others about it. We agreed I would give it a try when the trainings occurred.

Last week the notice came out about software trainings for the program. Over all, it was a time requirement of five hours. I thought that was quite a lot but kept my mouth shut. Then extraordinarily confusing emails came–but no response to questions–about signing up for training times. On top of five hours, I thought the general organizational confusion was not a good sign and it would be better if I got out before I got too frustrated. So I resigned.

I decided the general disorganization and lack of clarity a problem plus time spent learning new software were probably indicative of a frustrating future with the organization for me. But I thought it especially a wrong approach for "seniors." I doubt that those kinds of things are even considered around here. I heard this week a quote from somebody's grandma "You can't clean the house if you're not in it." I once was willing to "stay in the house" and try to make it work, but no more.

Clearly, I don't "fit in." I found my resignation sad because I was willing to volunteer a number of hours and my skills are such I could have been very helpful. But what

I'm not willing to do is spend time for the sake of spending time nor jump through hoops that I consider a waste of time. Feels like what they used to call "busy work." I never was very patient about it, but now have none. It seems to me that lots, including this program for "Aging" assume the myths are true and what older people have on our hands is a lot of time which we don't mind them filling up because what are we doing anyway but piddling about and deteriorating? Obviously, there are probably some people like that. But many are not and it seems to me, that there needs to be a greater respect for aging people's time, like there might be for younger people. Recently, somebody told me I wasn't retired.! What they meant, I guess, was that I didn't sit on a porch all day resting and doing nothing–a definition of retirement that is old hat if it ever existed. I like to create things and write and teach. That's what I did then; that's what I do now. The difference is I don't get paid for it now. I expect I will be doing that as long as I live.

I think you and Eve are good examples of the difference and that, unfortunately, the norms, assumptions and myths of aging reflect Eve and not the fact that there are plenty of different kinds of people, some doing great things and continuing their curiosity about the world, enjoying the present and even looking toward a future–including you.

I found it sad that Joan, as you said, helped her husband and her father, but it was not until after their death that she found her own voice and also helped other women. Better late than never, of course, but did it have to take so long? I know a woman here just like that–she is bright, funny and capable. But the work she did for decades enabled her husband to publish a number of books, all published under HIS name, not even with her as co-writer. Unlike Joan, she has not published anything since his death.

The white roses tradition about death, you mentioned at your facility, is another "better that than nothing," notice but such a distant, careful one–intending, I guess, to be non-intrusive. It's like "we want you to know that somebody has "passed" but we don't want to bother you about it much." I suppose the theory is they "fill in" with memorial services and the like. If I were the Director I'd be asking the residents, quite directly how they want to handle things now? Leave it the same or? I feel very strongly that some physical object, like a book, scrapbook could be made about the person–that is the art therapist in me. Then I'd put them on a special place on a shelf. I imagine that such a facility as yours would not like the physical stack of books getting bigger and bigger. But I strongly believe there should be some ritual (whatever the family does) at the place. It doesn't have to be much, but a marking that that person was part of the community and that there has been a loss. What do YOU think?

You asked about my divorce and my living alone. I divorced about 28 years ago–our children had left and we grew apart. I have lived alone since then–both in L.A. and here on Whidbey Island. Folk singer James Taylor said "You have to have some loneliness to have freedom." I only occasionally have felt loneliness over the years and mostly like living alone. I don't think I would like it as much though without living with a dog–which I have done all along. They greet you when you come home, want to be near you, but don't make demands like a human. For a while, I had a love who would come to visit for a few hours or a few days and then leave. At first, that was very tough for me because I was used to my husband being around most of the time. But then I began to recognize this pattern as the best of all possible worlds. Being really close for a short time and then letting go. I remember way back when, I went to visit another love for about a few days. When I got there he was depressed; when I left, he felt better and *I was* depressed. At that point I knew I probably couldn't live with anybody again.

I like living alone for many reasons, but two big ones. The first is I can run my life and my home exactly as I want it and be as "weird" as I want to be. I don't have to take anyone else into consideration (except the doggy, who doesn't demand much but food and love.) Of course, the other side of it is, I have no one but me to take care of me (and the house.) Like most women (and therapists) I was trained to be a caretaker and that part of me tends to kick in when there are other people, kids, guests etc. around. Can't help it. My boundaries get expanded and are permeable. I do like being with people and I think I even have a talent for friendship and that people don't generally find me unfriendly–but I can find enough of that in my "outside" life without living with it.

The second major reason I like living alone is that it is quiet and peaceful and I can be all the introvert I want. I can listen to my own inside voices instead of fielding those coming in from outside. I am a curious person and curiouser and curiouser and get to indulge that urge when I don't have input coming in from others. As you know, I have written a lot and made art. I also do yoga, see friends and read–mostly in the bathtub. I love movies and watch TV–sometimes to understand the culture. I play the TV sometimes for company. (I enjoy TV's meaningless noise. Unlike movies, TV writing is about words, not images–cause people often don't look at the picture.) I like having open time. Even on Whidbey, which is more simple than city living, things still break down, boringly and need attending to–e.g. I just spent half an hour on the phone with Customer Service at Amazon trying to pay for a pair of Jeans I bought (certainly an irony that wanting to pay is so tough.) It's what I call the "Relentlessness of Life Department"–that no matter how simple it seems; life keeps coming at 'ya.

Have to go. Having a friend for tea today and need to take the bagels out of the freezer and pick up a few things. Much love,
Max

June 23, 2016
Dear Max,

Not a particularly exciting subject, but I wanted you to know I am OK and hope you are well. I had planned to work on our book last week, but never made it. Doctors checking on my face, (improving slowly), general annual checkup-report good, and the death of a dear man, who with his wife befriended me when I came here. After her death two years ago, another mutual friend and I continued to arrange and play bridge with him– and we watched him decline. No memorial service is planned by his children, so the funeral served as closure for me.

One good experience: I visited my 100 year-old friend, Eve, to have her read what I had written about her in my email to you. Max, she chuckled through it and loved it. Then asked if she could read the rest of that letter. Max, she started to cry when she was reading what I wrote about Len. I was a little uncomfortable with that, but when she finished, she said it was beautiful and not to change a word. Do you agree? I don't want to make people cry. Her daughter (Professor of Anthropology) was there, read that letter and said she really liked our format.

I am committed to do some work for the Residents Council and should complete it this weekend. Fortunately, my term is up in December and when I grow up I hope I learn to keep my mouth shut and say NO.

One last good thing, before I go back to what I am avoiding: I do try to read a little before going to sleep. I just finished reading a book called *The Gurnsey Literary Society and Potato Peel Pie*. I had no idea about it, but quickly saw that the whole book is written as letters between several people. I loved the story; I loved the format–it was an easy, and delightful read. I would send it to you but it is on my Kindle.

When I finish what I have to do, I promise, promise to write my next letter. Also, just spoke to two residents here who were rescued from the Nazis. One man, was taken with 20 boys by the Rothchilds to London and a woman here as a small child was sent in a group of 50 children, to Sweden. Both very interested in talking to me about living here.

Enough.

Sending much love,

Myra

June 23, 2016

Dear Myra,

Interesting! We must really be on the same wavelength. Just now, downstairs for lunch—I had frozen burritos– I was thinking about you and then came upstairs to get at my computer again and there was your newsy email. Good, always, to know how you are and what you are thinking and doing. Stop feeling "guilt" about any of it–you do things as you can and so do I and I am beginning to think we should include (edited, of course) the newsy letters to each other, as well as the more "formal" ones. I am very glad you are ok–and not, as my mother used to start her phone calls—"what's new and awful?"

As to your friend Eve being moved and crying about what you wrote: I think that is terrific. What I want for us is that we "calls it the way we sees it"—and I think we are both pretty direct and do not skirt reality. If that moves people to tears sometimes, so much the better! All my life, I have been easily moved—like over dog TV commercials. But now in "old age"—and I don't know when it started, I just cry and cry. Not usually, going about daily stuff, or when I am with someone else, but when I am alone looking at TV or reading—receptively I guess. It's just how I am these days. I always thought being "vulnerable" was a good thing for a therapist. So many close off and get "burnt out" as a reaction, I guess, to all the ghastly stuff you hear.

As you may know, what we are doing is called an "epistolary novel –or book—which means a book of letters or documents. Here I thought we'd invented it. The first known was in the 1500's I think!

And speaking of all that, I was very upset over the Orlando massacre. And then they replayed and replayed it on TV. TV news plays on the power of imagery—it isn't the words you remember; it's the images you can't forget. I turned off the news every time it came on and watched more Kardashian trash than I ever have in my life, my form of denial. My adorable gay son is, thankfully, in Brazil for his research project. Brazil certainly has its troubles, but it isn't that as far as I can tell. Uggg. I have been working on my drawing of the Charleston massacre. Had it framed prematurely. (Had to take it out of the frame to work on it some more.) And I have an idea for awful Orlando drawings. I've been working on mass murder paintings and drawings for 15 years now. At the beginning, no one wanted to look at them. Unfortunately now, I think they might be "popular." Horrible![12]

Fun? An old friend came to visit. My husband and he met as grad students at UCLA in our 20s. He got a Ph.D., I think in Physiology, but was always an artist too. In grad school days he used to make terrific fish prints. He created and kept going all these years "Ornament Magazine." Up

---

[12] MBJ: I am working on a book tentatively called *An art psychotherapist considers mass murders, violence and mental illness*. It will contain my artwork on the subject.

until about two years ago, his son lived in the house in West Los Angeles that was my husband and my first house after our marriage (which we rented for $85 a month.) We were living there when I had my first child and I can remember sitting on the yellow couch, feeding her, and watching the sun come up.

He was "lost" for many years, but we reconnected when he came to my x's memorial service. We have had an email relationship since. Now he looks like a grey haired twinkly old man, but he was, like always, playful and funny. Have to end, because need to get to the market—one of my least favorite chores—and one of the worst things about the divorce—my husband used to do it.

Much love,

Max

July 8, 2016

Dear Max,

I am so glad for you that you finally finished the Con Safos book [*Voices from the Barrio*]. For someone who calls herself a "technological ninny," it is amazing that you are considering self-publishing. That is an enormous task. As computer literate as I consider myself, I took an easier route for the publishing of my last book. I found a publisher that Prints on Demand, which is also considered a form of self-publishing. The author keeps the copyright and the final word and the royalties are much higher than usual.

I was amused by your comparison of "gadgets" to bridge. Surprisingly, I don't see many women here playing with Tablets or I Pads. I know there are not many that even have computers. It seems that the couples that move in often have computers but one or the other uses it–rarely both. I see as many ordinary cell phones as I phones and more men than women seem to have them. Coincidently, just today, I was painting in the art room and one of the men passed by, saw me and decided to come in and kibbitz. He told me he just had a precious Face Time on his tablet with his two great granddaughters. He seemed surprised that I knew about Face Time and what it is. We are living here in a generation where the men still think women are not electronic age savvy. And I think they are, with few exceptions, right. I am considered, shall I say, unusual? More like an oddity. I try not to talk about what I have done or what I do. Why? Another story.

But card playing is incessant. Actually there are fewer bridge players than there are Canasta, Ma Jong and

Poker players. There are also Dominos, and a Scrabble foursome. The card game players are mostly women, a few couples and fewer single men. I suspect the women you are referring to in your community do live independently. In this kind of community having a steady game is the norm. It is the quickest way to meet people and get into a social group. Going to a "good" lecture, an excellent music appreciation program, is sitting and listening, not socializing. These activities are poorly attended. I continue to be amazed that every month, for the past two and a half years, about 50 people attend the Women's Club luncheon that I and two other women started. And so is management surprised, which continues to provide a lovely free lunch. I realize the initial attraction was the free lunch and socializing with different women at a table for 8-10. No reservations taken. But over the years, I think the women are as surprised as I and my committee that they enjoy the presentation (I arrange pro bono) and stay at least a half hour after lunch–often longer to ask questions and speak to the presenter. The presenters I engage are mostly artists, writers and musicians from the National League of American Pen Women and are my colleagues in that group.

I also think the women you are referring to are younger than the women who choose to live in a retirement community. We have 200 people in the "Independent Living" community and the average age is around 85. There are some 90+ and very few in their 70s. I think they are "managing their time" just as you and I do, albeit differently. And, yes, we are among the few that have driven our own courses.

Most of my peers here are used to doing what was expected, of them–marry, have children, keep house. And yes, you can be part of a couple and make your own decisions. But I think, Max, for our generation, it was not common nor easy and certainly not expected. My going back to college at 35 years old, mother of three daughters, ages 10, 8 and 7 years old was a decision we made before Len and I married. Actually, it was a proposition I made to Len when we realized that if we married while he was in medical school, I would have to work if we wanted to be independent of our parents. That meant I would give up my chance for an art scholarship and work until he graduated and completed his internship. I offered to do that if he would promise to make it possible for me to go to that art school when we could afford it. He not only promised, but during the years Len was establishing his practice and I was taking care of babies and doing all the things a young doctor's wife was supposed to do, he arranged for me to have one afternoon free every week to paint with a local artist.

I remember when I told my parents my decision to marry; they were heartbroken that I was not going on to college, but they respected my decision. Len's parents were appalled. His mother was certain that I would get pregnant and they would have to support us. Of course we didn't tell his parents of our future plans and she adored our daughters when they arrived, satisfied I was doing what I was supposed to do. But she was horrified when we told her I was going back to college–especially an art college. She was certain the neighbors and Len's patients would think he wasn't making a living. I promised I would never let the neighbors see me leave or come home in jeans and a paint shirt. My parents, of course, were thrilled. My father, I learned, had wanted to be an artist but that wasn't acceptable to his tough Hungarian father. My father died suddenly of a massive coronary, at age 53, the day after we told him our plans for my future studies. I have always been so glad that he knew.

Speaking of parents, Max, yours were amazing. And you were very clear about what you wanted to do–and did it. I have read your mother's biography and know both your parents were involved in the theatre. Compared to my very young parents, your mother and father were much more educated and very sophisticated. Their response to "your living in sin" was certainly not typical of their generation and I suspect your mom also was a young woman who drove her own course. And you, my dear friend, were far more daring than I was.

But we both know a few of our colleagues of our generations who were as determined to take charge of their lives as we were and still are. Since living here, I have come to know several women who would fit my earlier description of "have beens" but who, at this advanced stage of their lives, have made independent decisions about how they want to live the rest of their lives.

The women I know best are those with whom I eat dinner every night. Our group of six evolved over the years, during which we all sat with different people and gradually gravitated to, what I unabashedly call "a diverse, interesting, intellectual group." We are on the list of reserved tables for six, are well known by the dining room staff who never suggest someone else join us. I confess, I enjoy our separateness at dinner. Five of us are widows and one has never married–she is gay. Anne is 87 years old, has been here almost seven years and actually, like us, has driven her own course since a young adult when she determined to live her way and make choices not very acceptable in those years. She became a high school teacher, teaching history and English, lived with her partner, whom she obviously adored, for over thirty years. She nursed her partner through a terminal illness, joined a grieving group and decided to get on with her life. But not alone. She chose this community as the place she needed and wanted for the rest of her life.

Anne and I met shortly after I moved here. We had a very interesting group of five at dinner and together mourned the loss of our three tablemates within the next two years. Anne was one of the women who started the Women's Club luncheons with me, and helped me write by-laws for the Residents Council. You know my story and I think we are probably the nucleus for this group as we gradually became six.

Lorraine moved here with her husband who was wheel-chair bound. They were my neighbors and I often chatted with them as we waited for the elevator. He passed away a little over a year ago and I noted Lorraine was eating with a new resident, Sue, also a recent widow. Socializing with them as we waited for available tables at dinner time, I learned Loraine's daughter had made a list of other Independent living communities for her to consider after her husband's death, but she said she was not moving. Lorraine has shared many stories from the years she was a wife and a mother of four and I think her life was determined by her husband's schedule and family's needs. But in her mid-eighties she finally determined her own future. Sue, likewise had planned to stay in her condo after her husband's death. She told me she got tired of shopping, cooking for herself and looking at the four walls. Her daughter wanted her to move more north where she lives. But two years ago, at 90, Sue chose to move here. While she did volunteer work, her life before was determined by her husband's schedule and family needs. Both Loraine and Sue traveled with their husbands and are very intelligent and worldly. A year ago we decided to become a foursome at dinner. Then about six months ago, Rose, who I had mentioned in another context, in my last letter, approached me and asked if she and her close friend, Sheila, could join us, making a table of six for dinner. It seems there was an unpleasant incident at their table and they wanted to sit elsewhere. Of course we welcomed them and frankly, the company of these five intelligent women is the interesting, social time of my day. We are by no means of the same opinion on everything and our discussions are lively and even sometimes heated–especially during this election year. But it is a time and place when and where I am in the company of other women who think independently and say what they think.

Through the Resident Council, I have come to know another woman, Ellen, who, at 45 went back to college, got a degree in Gerontology and a Master's degree in Activities. She worked for a while as an Activity Director in a nursing home. Her husband became ill and after his death, she realized living in an apartment in a country club community as a widow, was not for her. She made the decision to move here; she is close to my age.

But sadly, Max, I know so many men and women who have literally been brought here by their children. And interestingly. I have seen that the single men prefer to sit with one or more women, rather than with a group of men. Thoughts?

I agree with you about Joan, but the journal she edited and put together here, was her publication and she had complete control of it. I think that was gratifying for her and as close as she could come to publishing her own work at that point in her life. I know, first hand, that not having something here to memorialize a deceased resident and offer closure leaves many residents feeling the loss longer than is necessary or useful at our age. The feeling of loss was pervasive when Joan died so suddenly and people (including me) still speak of her and her contributions. It certainly would have helped if the Activities Director had continued her journal but she didn't and we don't think she will. Anne and I have talked about taking it over when I am off the Council the end of this year. The Executive Director thinks that is a wonderful idea.

The fact is, Max, that not many staff in these communities are informed about the dynamics of the aging population. I think what is going on with the new program in your community is a perfect example of this. It sounds like a good program but the people in charge don't seem to have a clue about how to organize it and certainly don't understand how confusing, frustrating and disappointing such waffling can be, especially for seniors.

Thank you for sharing a little about your divorce. I hadn't remembered how long ago it was but did recall that for a time you did have another love. Your comments about not living with anyone again–and why– are definitely you. I wonder if that also reflects the difference between being widowed or divorced. I think, in the end, it is an individual decision based on what kind of marriage it was, what kind of person you are. Your talents. skills and accomplishments are so tremendous and varied you don't need someone to entertain you, stimulate you or even keep you company. But you are not anything typical of our generations.

We have agreed that most women in our generation identified themselves as the "wife of so and so" and did what was expected of them. And I think that we would agree that most men expected that as their due as the "supporter" of their family. And I see those identities still prevail here among single widows and widowers. Some do gravitate to each other, take all their meals together, attend activities together. And of course there is always a little gossip from a few wondering just how intimate they are. I think it is delightful that these little romances flourish and understand the loneliness that drives them. Len and I could be in separate rooms for hours, doing our own thing, one of us out and looking forward to getting home. It has been almost five years since he died and I still feel that empty space. I do keep my distance, but I confess, I have wondered how I would respond if one of the more appealing men made an effort to come closer.

Your comments about why you like to live alone resonated with me just this morning. Today is Sunday. I take my time getting up, enjoying the fact there are no meetings here that I should attend, no doctor's appointments, no activities that interest me and no bridge game for me. I take my breakfast to the patio along with the "New York Times" and shower and get dressed whenever I feel like it. Usually Sunday afternoon is a time I catch up on email and paperwork I may need to do. Having immersed myself in the Democratic convention this week I made finishing this letter to you today my priority. As I was getting dressed, and thinking about your last letter I suddenly realized how annoyed I would be if I had to attend to another person's wishes or needs. The schedule here demands I stop for dinner at 4pm. Until then I am independent and enjoying every minute.

Much love,

Myra

September 6, 2016

Dearest Myra,

I have been thinking at age 79 about having the freedom to talk about death and my dying, if I wish–and making it just one of those things that flits through the mind and that I'd like to share with someone. Perhaps people long married can do that; but as a single person, I have felt I had to watch my tongue and my thoughts with my grown kids, who get very anxious when I do, and with most of my friends, who seem to live as close to denial as they can. What got me thinking was my old friend of 50 years, Kurt, being here, now age 73. It is true that he is a minister and has been thinking about aging in those terms–so he might be something of a "special case" but the fact is, it was one of the many things we talked about not obsessively and freely. It felt good to be able to do it without censorship or filter and not have the other person become hideously anxious. And I'm so glad I can talk about it with YOU.

I am probably one of those people who has considered death a part of life for my whole life. My mother used to say "you can have that when I die," and certainly the potential of death has been part of me since I was 30 when my father died suddenly. Maybe it was because my beloved father had a major heart attack before he was 40 (and I was about 10) and although he lived much longer, death has definitely been visible for me for as long as I can remember.

I have had what I consider quite a truthful relationship with my adult children–no secrets, no hidden agenda and the ability to interact about what is important to us. But I've come to understand that they don't really want to hear about that part of me–perhaps the thought of my dying is simply too anxiety provoking for them. So I have consciously stopped talking about that part of my thinking with them. Friends generally don't consider it a topic of conversation–and if they are not denying it as much as possible, it is simply not something "appropriate" for conversation–even with the ones I have deep, open and profound friendships. Something about darkness and secrets that should remain background. There IS one friend, age 87, that it is possible to be open about death with–perhaps because she is older or perhaps because she is specifically her. I wonder if it is different where you live? I tend to think death is more present and in the forefront there–and what do you think about all this? How do your Independent Living colleagues see it?

I have even had a fantasy of holding a group called something like "Death and Dying"–I bet quite a few people would show up for something like that–where such a subject is defined and "outside" everyday life. (It seems to me that it is more difficult when talk about death feels more "accidental" in a conversation than when it is specifically planned for and defined with boundaries. E.g. on Wednesdays I go to the "Death and Dying" group.) There is more and more in the current culture, thankfully, about the practical aspects of planning–but is there somewhere for the OTHER stuff, the more emotional stuff. Not that I know of. I am reminded of other cultures where death is more in the forefront–such as Mexico where one day of the year as part of the "Day of the Dead" events, people actually go to the cemetery and picnic there to be with the ancestors. And the observant Jews, of course, who wait for a year, if I remember correctly, to put a headstone with the name on the grave. America these days is such a "moving on" (and away?) kind of culture!

As a Jew, I am an Atheist and don't believe in an afterlife. It is all here and now for me. I sometimes wish I did believe, because I think that believing there is something after is comforting to many. Many believe that, I think. I listen to the language–so many say "passed" instead of "died" as if one were passing into another phase of life. It is a "softer" word, but it doesn't imply any kind of end. And I am interested that there is no word that says "death" for dogs at all–"putting down," "euthanizing" etc. Was it psychologist Rollo May who wrote about warding off death as a powerful force within life and the impetus for creativity? There have been many writers and artists who spoke about artistic creativity coming to be because of the recognition of death as an ending, and creative expression potentially being some sort of immortality.

I deeply believe in concepts of "meaning." And most of these throughout my life have been posed against the recognition that one day it will end. Perhaps I am more aware of death than most, but that's how it is.

Love,

Max

September 8, 2016

Dear Myra,

I reread your last long email to me again in preparation for writing this one, and I was fascinated with your description of your life in your Independent Living facility. It occurred to me that I would love to know the stories of those particular women you treasure and sit with at dinner, as to their thoughts and feelings about their lives as women in this culture of ours and especially now in their later years.

By the way, I appreciated your telling me of your early years with Len and giving up your art scholarship for his endeavors. I think your "bargain" with him about your own schooling before marriage is unusual for a woman of that time and generation. Already you were asserting your own individual needs–that you had them and wanted to be able to fulfill them. Hurrah– that's the Myra I love. Actually, I didn't do that–maybe it was my self-esteem at the time–-surely I followed my own path, but it wasn't "ours" nor anything acknowledged nor planned for between us–and in my time, what you did was what your husband wanted and did, plus having kids, not what YOU wanted. Someone said "you gave it all up for your husband's career." I too gave up two other art scholarships for graduate school that I was awarded when I graduated from Scripps. I married at 21, in London after our year on motorcycles and took the scholarship to UCLA because my husband was becoming a graduate student in Physiology there. I was awarded three, but took the one where my husband had chosen to go. That's what a wife did then. I became a Teaching Assistant in the Painting Department and I remember I had to sign a loyalty oath (about 1961) to do so. Distasteful as it was, I rationalized that we really needed money—which we did.

The painting department at UCLA was almost all men faculty in those days and the two women in the department were regularly derided. (One knew more about most things than all the men combined and the other painted flowers.) It was very sexist—Feminist and artist Judy Chicago who was there at that time and has written about it. As an undergrad at Scripps I was told I painted "like a man" which was intended as the highest compliment, but in my first meeting at UCLA, my faculty advisor said to me "Your painting is all tricks!" I didn't have much idea what he meant, but I knew it didn't feel good. I eventually left UCLA before earning an MFA because of what I now recognize as overt sexism. I consider my leaving an important turning point and my life might have been very different if I had felt able to take one of those other art scholarships. Thankfully, I think the possibilities and opportunities for women are different these days and vastly more open. I have worked hard to make that openness happen. My daughter who is a TV writer tells me that of TV writers, 19% are women.

It was to my husband's credit that he supported me in doing what I needed when I followed my art bent as I almost went crazy just raising a child. I used to "sneak out" to attend an art class once a week–and it FELT like sneaking out. When I started social work school at the age of 30, it was my son's first day in kindergarten and the mothers (not the fathers, of course,) were supposed to come to class. My husband did. His support was probably the big thing that enabled me to stay in the marriage as long as I did. But he was the one seen as beneficent and I was the one who felt the guilt. I remember humorist James Thurber's comment, "A woman's place is in the wrong." Roles are more open, thankfully these days, but I know there's misogyny and sexism still some around.

I remember, for example, the female therapist who told us as a couple we had "role reversal" which she clearly considered a problem in our relationship and pathology even. (He cooked and did a lot of the child care.) On the other hand, I remember the time in our house in Mendocino when Douglas spent the day cooking some very complicated recipe from "Sunset Magazine" for a dinner we were having for some friends that night. The people came. The food was served. It was attributed to him and was excellent. The guests said to me "Thanks, Maxine–dinner was very good." I said "I didn't do it, Douglas did!" As we stood at the door to say goodnight to our guests, they said again "Thanks, Maxine so much for such a good dinner." They simply couldn't register that Douglas had made it; a man cooking was not something that was part of the compartmentalized male role or in the thinking of other people!

What I want to think about with you in this letter, however, is what you said: "The fact is, Max, that no staff in these communities know about the dynamics of the aging population." You continued, talking about the program getting started here on Whidbey that I told you about: "It sounds like a good program, but the people in charge don't seem to have a clue about how to organize it and certainly don't understand how confusing, frustrating and disappointing such waffling can be especially for seniors." BRAVO, Myra.

We got started with this book in the first place because we both understood how little was known about this particular generation–75 years old plus. I have often called them "social pioneers" because I don't believe anyone has been this way before. Along with how little is understood. There are many assumptions and myths– believed by many aging themselves! Like, it's all about loss of faculties and friends and etc. Unquestionably, some is– but then some is not! For example, I recently saw some friends that I knew in my twenties, then lost for about 50 years.

Admittedly, they looked a bit different, older–and so do I, but I didn't find them different at all as personalities. Even their voices sounded the same. They remain the people they always were–curious about the world and the future and humorous.

I remember hearing recently about a research study conducted on over 75s at an Assisted Living Facility. It reminded me of the time in the 70s, in Social Work school at USC. For my thesis, I was doing research on Orthodox and Secular Jewish women and I was reading all the literature available. I discovered that there was a lot of literature on Orthodox women and virtually none on Secular women. The obvious reason was that the researchers COULD FIND the orthodox women, in synagogues and Jewish neighborhoods and the like, but by definition, the secular women were more integrated into diverse communities and therefore harder to find and research. But the researchers of Orthodox women generalized their findings to ALL Jews.

I was reminded of this by the Assisted Living research. Obviously, some of the findings probably also pertain to people who *do not* live in AL, but–also obviously–some does not. I may be wrong on this, but as I remember, aging is seen as negative generally. (I get humorous quotes all the time from people I know about how difficult aging is, and sometimes emails describing aging sent by a person that says it isn't like this at all.) As everybody knows there are tremendous differences in Jews– even Jewish atheists– there is a tremendous difference, of course in Seniors.

I for one, do not feel negative but am smarter and curious about what comes next. I also like that certain traits which might have been considered "weird" in a younger person are thought, at worse, to be "eccentric" in older. Older people feel more free to be themselves and act as they wish, somehow cutting loose from society's norms. One of the great things about growing older is the broad extent of leeway given and the ability to be yourself as you choose to be. I wouldn't want to be young again for anything.

The program I was telling you about, first required volunteers to learn a new software program, then sent out days and times for meetings to learn it, then sent out an email that said they hadn't meant those as *real* times and it was "like herding cats" to get this all organized. (I was insulted.) A friend of mine paid a yearly membership, was visited by a volunteer and when she said that she wanted to get the battery changed in her fire thing, was told they didn't do that (nor was she given a referral to somebody who did.) That "sort of thing" was specifically what she had joined for. Then she was sent a rather nasty letter, by mistake, six months early, saying she needed to send in her yearly membership fee. And there were nasty follow-up letters too–all mistakes. I think this kind of disorganization is accepted because it is thought that aging people get things mixed up and can't remember anything? I find it inexcusable.

Isn't it better to approach this aging generation, the over 75s, with a NOT KNOWING attitude–open to the many possibilities there may be. The constructed lenses through which many view the world do not allow for difference. We can still be taught, can't we? And, in my opinion, it is the over 75s that can teach us, if we can be open to seeing and hearing them.

Love,

Max

October 6, 2016

Dear Max,

Another adventure in independent living!

I am writing this and watching TV as it charts the path of Hurricane Matthew, due to hit here within the next two hours. It is now called a Category 4 Monster Hurricane. Fortunately, last night my daughter, Bonnie, brought me to her home–an apartment on the 5th floor of a very solid building. But listening to staff yesterday, explain the schedule and preparations for the residents of the facility, was a study in angst. The management explaining their responsibility for the safety of staff, as well as residents who, by then, were anxious. Residents were nervous and confused. Breakfast and lunch would be served today, but the dining room would be closed at 2pm. Sandwiches would be available to take to apartments and any food served for breakfast and lunch would be boxed to go. Everyone must remain in their apartments during the hurricane. The generator serves one elevator in each of the three buildings (we have two in each) and keeps lights on in main rooms on first floor. It does not protect loss of power in the apartments. Batteries and flashlights were available for purchase at the front desk. As I left with others, at the end of the meeting, the anxiety was palpable.

As the current secretary of the Resident Council, I know we have approximately 190 residents in this community. Most are single and there are no more than ten couples. The majority use walkers or canes and 10-20 have aides–depending on state and progression of medical problems. This does not include residents in the Assisted Living section which is on two floors of one building. My community is a large one and very few have family close by. Most remained during the storm.

I stayed at my daughter's home for three days and two nights. As you probably read, South Florida was very lucky and we escaped serious damage. We did have bouts of torrential rain and power outages, but there was little serious flooding. When I returned home to my apartment in the facility, I learned that management did a wonderful job feeding everyone and answering all calls of concern and anxiety. Most of the staff was sent home but top management slept here and truly "minded the stores" and the residents.

What they didn't realize is the very thing you and I have been talking about: They just didn't understand that waiting until the day before to tell everyone what the "plan" would be, created a high level of anxiety and even initial anger. Hurricanes are common here and plans should be in place for residents to see when they move in. Many of us choose to live here to feel SAFE and to be taken care of in just such a threat to our environment.

This is not the first time I have experienced this kind of last minute decision-making and announcements. I have been here now five years; Three years ago, when threatened with a hurricane, we were told just a day before that there would be cots in the auditorium and residents could decide if they wanted to bring three days' supply of medicine, change of clothing, stay there or remain in their apartment and food would be delivered. I assumed this was the "Hurricane Crisis Plan" and told people this when, as a Council member, I was asked what we were supposed to do. I am sure I contributed nothing to calming anyone when we kept hearing from staff "Everything would be announced soon!"

Back to you and me. We both supported our husbands first, as we were expected to. But we also knew what we wanted and made sure we got it. Len and I often referred to "our agreement." Nevertheless, I had a few neighbors who managed to remind me how lucky I was that my husband "allowed" me to go back to college. My mother-in-law implied the same and was concerned that neighbors would think that he wasn't making a living if he was "sending" me back to college. Of course, that reflected her generation's views of women and men's roles in society.

I can empathize with your frustration about the sexist attitude at UCLA. I went to a private, all-girls art college in Philadelphia, Moore College of Art–one of the oldest in the country. It is still an excellent school and still all girls, in spite of many tries to break the charter. So I didn't encounter sexism until I became a faculty member in a medical school.

But four interesting things happened at Moore relevant to male/female roles back in the sixties: Each year we had a different, well-known local artist as our painting professor. At the end of the first year, that professor asked if he could do a portrait of me. I was floored, then flattered and agreed. He did a lovely drawing of me which Len and I both liked and he gave it to me. During my years at Moore, he remained friendly and very supportive and we often chatted about our families. (I still have that drawing among many of my paintings.)

In my second year, the professor, a single good-looking man around my age, asked me to have lunch with him every day. I asked him why in the world would he want to have lunch with me, a married woman with three children, when he was surrounded by so many gorgeous young women? It was 1960. He told me he was gay and had decided I would not be uncomfortable knowing this and he trusted me. This was not something that he could talk about. I did eat lunch with him whenever I could; my young fellow students kept their distance.

He and his partner became part of our family. His partner was an architect and both men were interesting company. With trepidation and much urging from us, they finally bought their dream house and moved in together. We remained close friends for years until Len and I retired to Florida and they moved into an independent living community. My children and I still have several of my professor's paintings hanging in our homes.

During my last two years at Moore, I experienced some of what you did at UCLA. In one professor's class, I probably did my most powerful and bizarre paintings from sheer frustration and anger. His method of teaching was to humiliate a student in his critique. My turn came when he used a painting I had just started to demonstrate "how NOT to start a painting;" not unlike your "your painting is all tricks." I went home and painted a huge abstract with slashes of black interspersed with green. My family hated it and one daughter titled it "Lady Macbeth coming through the door." I took it into class for an assignment and, of course, he thought it was very good. Near the end of that year, this same man asked me to come to his office at the end of the day. I no longer remember what he said, but I do remember telling Len about this strange conversation. My dear husband laughed and told me my teacher was "hitting on me." If I had the time, this is when I might have transferred out.

In my last year, I was required to take a course in 3-dimensional design and complete a wood sculpture as a final project. I was told by the Dean that the professor thought I was a "rich doctor's wife taking art classes as a hobby." But to be fair, he was going to ask another faculty member to grade my work without knowing my name. I got an "A." But by the time I got to Hahnemann Medical College as an adjunct professor and head of the new art therapy program, the very first art therapy graduate program in the country, all of this male acting-out prepared me for the good old boys' club of tenured professors. I was given a great two-room office–the outer one set up like a lab where patients could paint and make art and the inside one I furnished like an office. And as a special gift, I was given the coffee pot for the floor–they said because I "had a sink." As you can imagine I made coffee for about three weeks and then somehow I just didn't have time in the morning. However, I was available to show anyone in need of coffee, how to make it. Max, in spite of the Feminist Movement, our male cohorts are the same today.

At Hahnemann, since I was available in the morning to teach people to make coffee, eventually I became "one of the guys." I was also appointed the first tenured woman professor in the Department of Psychiatry. Within five years, there were at least ten women promoted to this rank throughout the graduate school, including two more in my department.

There was another interesting and relevant encounter I had with this faculty of male professors. It was during the time that NOW[13] was fighting for equal pay for equal work for women. I don't think you know this, but coincidentally it was also during the seven years that my daughter Marsha, the incredible lawyer for juveniles, took time out from that career, applied for and became the Legal Director for NOW. So along with fighting sexual harassment of women in the workplace, discrimination against women seeking employment and deadbeat fathers, she was also embroiled in the equal pay issue.

Naturally, since there were so few women as faculty at Hahnemann, we women professors got to know each other and shared stories and actually got Marsha to come speak to us We also learned, by sharing those stories, that we women professors were all making $10,000 less per year than our male colleagues. Needless to say, we all began planning department protests.

The psychology professor in my department suggested I speak to our Chairman, but I felt I could not because I had just fought for and succeeded in getting substantial raises for the individual Directors of the three

---

[13] NOW is the National Organization for Women

programs I coordinated. As I heard the story later, (reported by both my colleague and our Chairman,) she went into see him. She waved a finger in his face and, in her strong Argentinean accent, told him that unless he did something to rectify this inequity, we were all calling Marsha. He told her (and me later) "Don't call Marsha!" This rare and wonderful man proceed to get us all $3000. salary increases for the next three years. So there were a few good guys.

Until moving here as a widow, I didn't pay much attention to male behavior, but I can't avoid being confronted with it here. For one thing, regardless of age or impairments, the men will hold onto their cars longer than the women–even if they must use a walker. There are those that are "nice" men, interested in who you are and what you did in your "previous life" and sharing their stories. (These are the best bridge partners.) There are those that obviously were macho young men and are now macho old men. And, perhaps because of the Feminist Movement, many couples come here when the woman falls ill and the man needs to be the care-taker. Role reversal today is much more common than it was when you and Douglas were married. And there are always those men, regardless of age or marital status, who are flirtatious and "hitting" on someone. And likewise, I see some of the women, especially if they need someone to fulfill their need to take care of someone, being flirtatious. But having learned to be "one of the guys" with the "good old boys" at Hahnemann, I have managed to steer clear of any complications in my relationships. I do play bridge with an amazing 99 year-old man, whose wife is lovely and have worked with several men on the Resident Council. And there is one man here who, actually, is a dear old friend from before.

After his wife died of cancer, he was living alone in their apartment and getting depressed. Some friends and his sons urged him to tour our facility and consider moving here. Last year while taking the grand tour, he saw my picture on the Resident Council bulletin board, said he recognized me and knew my married name. He asked the staff person to call me and tell me to come down. I did, and had a tearful reunion with Lou (as I will call him.)

We grew up in the same neighborhood and hung out together from the time I was six years old until we both moved away when we were teenagers. He was the same age as Len, knew him and went all through school with him, from kindergarten to 12th grade. He told me that "'none of the guys' could believe you really got married."

He did move here and one night at dinner, stopped at our table and gave me a picture of Len he had cut out of his Junior High School year book. I always enjoy our bumping into each other in the dining room and hallways. He stops, says a few friendly words, and tells anyone around how long he has known me.

I think people don't change; we just become "more of what we were. And that, Max, I think is the crux of what you wanted to discuss in this letter. Unfortunately, I think this awareness and knowledge of personality development is missing in our staff and administrators. You said you recognized the same personalities in old friends you hadn't seen for years. In another 10-15 years, I believe you would see those same personalities more defined, exaggerated, muted, depending on their circumstances and health.

I agree there is a difference in Assisted Living compared to Independent Living. People who are in Assisted Living have physical impairments and care is supervised by registered nurses. This staff is trained to address the physical needs and understand the emotional ramifications of this population. But, as you found in your own research, there are differences in how one handles illness in old age and how one handles aging regardless of where they are living "independently." At the end of your last letter you ask "Isn't it better to approach the over 75s with a NOT KNOWING attitude, open to the many possibilities there may be?" And you suggest that by being open to seeing and hearing the population they can teach us about these differences. I agree and disagree. While we were determined that our book would not be a text book, we are in fact, asking to be seen and heard in our differences and in teaching our readers. But administrators, staff and people who deal with 75+s, taking care of our aging population in neighborhoods and independent living communities cannot take on these tasks with a NOT KNOWING attitude: THEY NEED TO BE INFORMED.

One of my earliest inspirations for wanting to write this book was Atol Gawande's *Being Mortal*, which we both read. His perspective on the lack of information regarding the over 75+ population was from the medical field and his examples were wonderful. His work wasn't a text book either, but it was an eye opener for practitioners and caretakers of the elderly. I think we can do the same.

Your thoughts?

Love, Myra

October 15, 2016

Dear Myra,

I loved your last letter, in all ways and want to tell you a story about my experience with salaries in the university. As you know, I taught for many years at Loyola Marymount University, a small institution in Los Angeles. When I began to teach there in 1980, I had a talk with myself about money. I knew, teaching in a private college, my salary would be less than at a public university and probably that there were many inequities between departments and between women and men. My new boss, Chair of my college, even told me "the women will be gone soon" despite the fact that it had been many years already since Loyola and Marymount had combined and become coed. So long ago, I determined NOT to fuss about my salary if I could help it. I thought it took too much time and energy. If I could help it, I would not regularly go to see the administration about salary inequities for women and my own. Many women I know did and were successful. Many I had encouraged to ask. But they had to ask. They didn't get just because it was "fair."

Since I am a good "compartmentalizer" and was married at the time to a man with a monthly salary, I was able to hold to my plan for more than 20 years, while I watched many male and female colleagues go into the Academic Vice President and ask for more salary. The women often asked on the basis of equity and often got. When I retired from LMU, the VP gave me a stipend for two years. I was surprised but gratefully accepted it, you can bet. A female dean who was a friend that I told the story to after I left called it "Guilt money."

Love,

Max

October 25, 2017

Dear Myra,

Thanks so much for calling me last night to "tell you I'm still alive." So sorry you and the others are having computer etc., Comcast problems. I wonder if it has to do with the storm. I've been watching Comcast for a long time. When I first moved to Whidbey Island, it was the only game in town if you wanted to watch TV. (It isn't any more.) I got so frustrated with Comcast once, I wrote to the CEO in Philadelphia and was surprised to get a phone call from an executive who was actually a big help. At the time they had gotten much publicity about their terrible customer service and everybody hated Comcast. With their attention to my letter, I assumed they were trying to do something about their awful image.

Since then, I have watched the company and asked questions of the tech guys who came to the house to fix one thing or another. They are always quite reliable and quite good–even on time, despite the fact that I can't get them directly but have to go through Comcast's customer service shenanigans in the Philippines to get them. As one tech said "We are the front line, so we hear everything and everybody yells at us." Recently when one came to install a new box, he said "We are making changes, but it will take years. He gave me a new remote. It is the most awfully designed thing, crammed with letters and numbers signifying nothing that I can understand. Not the usual bad design, but much worse. Where is Steve Jobs now that Comcast needs him? But enough about that.

What I have been thinking about in this horrendous election season is the loss of the American Dream and people's anger over it. I remember first recognizing this loss as a major psychological crisis for the country somewhere in the 1980s when college kids could no longer afford housing and were coming back in droves to stay with their parents. I remember thinking then that it was the end of the American Dream where we know in our guts that our children will do better than we did. I thought it was a huge psychological wrench and a loss of hope.

(Note: this letter was never finished. The U.S. Trump versus Clinton presidential election intervened. Like many people, I was stunned, destabilized and stopped by the election. The unfinished letter remains in my Drafts folder to this day.)

November 3, 2016

Dearest Max,

I just wanted to let you know I am OK and working on page 2 of my letter to you. I am always amazed at the memories and thoughts your letters evoke. I had a (literally) very shaky two weeks and finally completed other stuff so I could enjoy doing our stuff.

My neuropathy is spreading up my lower legs and into my fingers, so I decided to see a well-recommended neurologist. He prescribed the "best" medicine. I took it that night, woke up in the morning and my room was spinning. I keep my walker near my bed and finally made my way to the kitchen and made a cup of coffee. It took a couple of hours for the dizziness to subside enough for me to get dressed and out. I decided to cut the pill in half and try it one more time. The next morning, no spinning–just going round and round. Did the coffee again and got moving in a couple of hours. I checked the internet and this is medication everyone recommends. Well, apparently, not for me. Also recommended for neuropathy is exercise. So I am on the stationary bike in our fitness center two nights a week and knitting a sweater for my great granddaughter. It took two weeks for the lightheaded and wobbly feelings to stop. I am back to my normal 92 years and trying to keep calm throughout this insane election period. The knitting helps with the TV too.

Much love,

Myra

November 4, 2016

Dearest Myra,

I'm so sorry about your *tsouris*[14] and thanks for letting me know. I wish I could do something! I had a back thing this week and actually hoped I had done something, rather than it was general decrepitude. (Luckily, it seems to have disappeared—yay.) For "balance and strength" I use a Peggy Cappy "easy yoga" DVD. I got it on Amazon. It has

---

[14] "Tsouris" is Yiddish for troubles.

a lot of simple standing-on-one-foot exercises and I think it has really helped me get stronger in the legs. When I started I was pretty shaky. Now, much more solid.

We will all be glad when the election is over. I think most everyone is feeling a kind of generalized depression and anxiety about it and sometimes not so generalized. For example, having already published the Con Safos book, this week the Con Safos guys want to make "corrections." Uggggg. I had an email melt down and hissy fit the other night and told them, among other things, that enough was enough. I'm not sorry I did it. It's like when teenagers push their parents to see where the limits are.

[Daughter] Alexa has just arrived in Boston, where her play "Fingersmith" is on in December at the American Repertory Theater. And [son] Ben finally managed to have a teaching day this week after more than 10 days of virus/weakness. Today, here, the sun is out after a week of heavy rain. I planted bulbs and today I feel I'll be around to see them come up. I'm also working on a letter for our book, for you—but I'm going to save these smaller ones. They are certainly about aging life–any life for that matter.

Much love,

Max

PART IV

2017

January 16, 2017

Dearest Myra,

I want to tell you about my thoughts about future planning that I discussed with Ben and Alexa when I spent Xmas with them. And I want your feedback and thoughts!

I have spent a good deal of time and energy in the last few years planning my finances, but at this point realized I hadn't thought through what I want my future years to be like. The fact is that I am fast running out of money and am again looking at having to sell the house, which is really my only financial asset. (It would have been sooner, except for my selling of the Horace Pippin painting a few years ago.) I think there is something about gender here and my divorce that was almost 30 years ago now. Someone long ago called it the "feminization of poverty," although I imagine that outliving your money may well be a problem for seniors of all genders and increasingly, as people live longer.

Thirty years ago, when I divorced in California, we divided up all our financial assets. I got half of his UCLA retirement to that date. So ironically, my half of his retirement is what I have been living on for years. My own pension at Loyola Marymount was much smaller and he got half of it. I do not regret that I worked "for love" but women's pay and the lack of equity with men is obviously coming back to bite me. To sell the house, I would have to do various things to put it in shape, like painting it and putting my things in storage which would cost money too. I figure I have money for about two more years here. I love my house and, if it weren't about money, wouldn't leave it. It also is the only real asset I have to leave to my children. But I'm a pragmatist too and if I have to, I have to.

But then I thought where do I want to be? Time to figure that out. Of course, I have no idea where my brain will be in a few years. Can't plan that too well, unfortunately. Space is not an issue with me; I can live in a small one with no problem. But where? Probably not here on Whidbey because it is too hard for my kids to get here. Los Angeles where I was born and grew up? No. Alexa is based there of course—but with her professional life, she really comes and goes a lot and where she'll end up is anybody's guess. Seattle? Can't think of a reason why and probably don't want to be in a city. Ben has often said I could live with him in Beacon, NY —and he said it again this time. I said "Ben: you don't want your mother living in the back room. You don't even <u>have</u> a back room!" The fact is, although I am very grateful for his generosity I don't want to live with him or anybody! In actuality, I think <u>you </u>have the right approach and are a good model: As I see it, you are in the same town with some of your kids who take you out, but you have your OWN LIFE. At this juncture, I am not interested in the facility part of how you've organized things and probably couldn't pay for it. But who knows, maybe in a while, it will be necessary. So I am trying to gather information and think through some things. (Like I have a little cottage on my property—could rent the big house and stay there, etc.) Maybe an apartment is an interim step. And I noticed that there are some assisted living places in Ben's town in the Hudson River Valley–but it is coooold there.

I wonder if you'd be willing to tell me how you came to the decisions you did. I think we are rather the same, in wanting to live our own lives. I think I'm going to call the Senior Center now and see what they can tell me about a consultant. Atol Gawande is coming to town to give a talk in early Feb.[15] I plan to go, so I can see him "in the flesh" and decide if he deserves the "feet of meat" award—for those idols whose feet do not turn out to be made of clay.

Love, Max

---

[15] It turned out Gawande was appearing via webinar which was cancelled due to storms on the east coast. It has not been rescheduled yet. So much for "in the flesh!"

Jan 16, 2017

Max,

I will answer both letters, be your first consultant. But first, I have to finish the pussy hat[16] I am making for my grand daughter-in-law who is marching with the women in Philadelphia on Saturday. Bonnie is mailing it Wednesday, with the one she is making for her daughter, who is marching in NY. We were sent the pattern by another granddaughter knowing we are the fast knitters.

Much love,

Myra

January 18, 2017

Dear Max,

The Pussy hat is done and gone.

So Max dear, you do not want to look at assisted living places, let's hope you will never need that.

What you may be interested in is an Independent Living Community. That is what I am living in, as you know. The first time I looked at these communities was in 2003. Karen and Marvin were retired here; Bonnie and Joel

---

[16] For the Women's Protest March, the day after Donald Trump's inauguration. "Pussy" refers to a statement of Trump's about grabbing women's pussies

had just bought a large house and were getting ready to retire here also. Len and I decided we were ready to sell our four-bedroom house, downsize to a two-bedroom apartment and let the girls handle guests.

Len had a substantial pension that was diminished as a result of poor advice from a so- called "reliable" source in Florida. Fortunately, I had a pension from Hahnemann and we both had Social Security plus a few solid investments. We were OK.

Before we decided on an apartment in Florida, Len asked if I wanted to look at Independent Living communities. I knew nothing about them, went on the internet and picked one close by to check out. After the grand tour, a look at the schedules, the shuffle board, the tellings about trips to doctors and lunch, I came home, had a strong martini and went to bed with a migraine–the first I had ever had. It was awful!! We moved to a lovely apartment and never mentioned that subject again.

In the meantime, some of our friends were moving to these communities and I learned there were big differences. We had visited one of the worst. When Len died, and I lost his social security check (ours were almost equal) I knew I would have to move. While the girls all offered that I come live with them, I knew that was out of the question-for all the reasons you said plus three sons-in-laws who were still my friends and I wanted to keep it that way. Bonnie and I started looking. First you have to decide how much money you can spend, how big a place you want or can afford: 1 bedroom, 2 bedrooms, efficiency, etc. Max, you have no idea how different these places are. We looked at eight, saw all kinds of apartments with all kinds of amenities. I didn't get migraines, but I did begin to feel depressed and anxious. What 'hooked' us here was that the marketing person took us into her office and asked me what I wanted. In seven previous places not ONE person ever asked me what I wanted.

Here, I got everything I wanted in a building that was a good walk from the main building, which I thought was good exercise. But five years ago I was only using a cane.

A person at one of the places we visited told me I was entitled to a widow's veterans' pension if my husband was in the army for at least five years. Len was, and I applied. It took 11 months to come through, but I got the maximum which was almost equal to his social security check.

By my third year here, I couldn't walk as well and was using a walker and I was now able to afford an apartment in the main building which was better for me. I didn't have to walk as much and the main building is where the facilities and dining room are. My apartment is still a one bedroom but a little bigger all around and a little more of what I want.

None of this changes the fact that retirement facilities are big business and there is everything good and bad about this environment. The one where I am at is not the best place around nor the fanciest, but I am comfortable, safe, secure and not a medical or financial burden to anyone. Last, I don't know what the prices are on the West coast, but I can afford what I pay here which includes rent, two meals a day, transportation within a 10-mile radius, nurses and emergency care 8-4pm including weekends. The fee here is considered "moderate." The more exclusive places charge more—about $6,000 and more for a couple. They offer 30 meals a month. Still it beats a one-bedroom condo, doing your own cooking and paying for transportation when you stop driving.

Hope this helps.

Love,

Myra

January 24, 2017

Dear Myra,

Thanks so very much for all your good and specific information. It really helps. I am sending it onto Alexa and Ben and will get back to you "formally" soon. FYI: I tend to use the words "Assisted Living" and "Independent Living" interchangeably and shorthand for a retirement facility, but I know there is a difference.

Thinking about you a lot these days. Having known you for a lot of years, I consider you (and this is a complement) a street fighter in all the best ways. One thing I like best is your relentless anger and high expectations and your pushing on. As women of this American culture, we are still expected to "look our best," not to mention the old saw "letting yourself go." Even though older people, particularly women, become invisible, we have internalized the cultural demands.

As you were looking at potential homes for you after Len's death, I thought the question "What do you want?" was so poignant, so right on, and unfortunately so seldom asked. I loved that you noticed it and noticed its omission in other facilities you looked at. A few years back, when I thought I would have to sell my house because I was running out of money to live on, I looked into a few "Retirement Homes." I looked at the one here on south Whidbey and a few others in Seattle and the "mainland" including one non-profit and one for retired academics–presumably heavy on intellectual pursuits. Judging from websites and information brochures, they were all about the same. All were expensive. I would have had to sell my house to have even a beginning of enough money.

As pretty much an introvert at this time of my life, I like my separateness–my writing and painting, and I don't play bridge. I want my interactions with people to have the potential to be meaningful. I grew up in a time and in a family where *conversation* was a pleasurable activity and now live in a world where deep, expanding and far-reaching conversation has all but disappeared. I value authenticity and have little interest in "small" talk, although I understand it as a form of social connection. I have spent a lifetime trying NOT to tell the truth when the market cashier asks "HOW are you?" I think my time is the most valuable thing I have and I don't want to waste it.

Although I like the things around me that have meaning to me–paintings, books, photographs and especially my folk art, living in a smaller space would not be a problem for me; I live a lot in my head anyway, and always have. I have thought the "Retirement community" format was not for me. There are too many rules and there is the unwritten assumption that many, many activities, filling up one's time so-to-speak, are a good thing. (In fact, one facility I inquired about, called me the following week to ask me to teach art.) At least it's not right for me now.

I have been living alone for a long time and even though there are sometimes difficult tradeoffs to that, I like it. I am long divorced and my grown children live their own lives in Los Angeles and New York. To be fair, perhaps if I had looked longer and deeper at retirement facilities, I might have seen the possibility for more individual differences, but as it was, I saw a kind of well-intentioned "crowd mentality."

Atol Gawande's viewpoint in his *Being Mortal* is that most seniors are placed in retirement facilities to assuage their children, because, quite naturally, they want their older parents to be safe. Safety is obviously an issue as one ages, but I believe that the multiple needs and wishes of older people cannot be generalized or lumped into one bag. That question, "What do you want?" is crucial. Safe caretaking is not enough for most people. The over 75 crowd are social pioneers that we haven't looked at yet. Looking away and putting them in "places" where they are safe reminds me of what they used to do with the mentally ill in "asylums." That is, a problem that cannot be solved should be humanely as out of sight as possible.

I look forward to hearing from you!

Love,

Max

February 7, 2017

Dear Max,

Bad news and good news. I am getting shingles on my chin and have referred pain in my ear. The response from the nurse and me is s–t–several times. The good news is I am in isolation for two days and should finish up my list of letters and get them off to you by the end of the week.

It has not been good here for several days. On top of everything else, my little city of Deerfield, Florida did routine testing of water last Friday and found E-coli in the water. We were warned to not even wash dishes in the water. Fortunately, Bonnie brought over a case of bottled water and the ban was lifted Sunday night. Since I was prepared, I waited to use the tap water until Monday night.

I certainly hope no one was careless–just what we all need, an epidemic of e-coli.

Off to lunch on my patio and then to work.

Love,

Myra

Feb 7, 2017

Dearest Myra,

I'll say it straight out: SHITTTTTTT and more shit! So very sorry. I sure hope the reality is less than the expectation. Hopefully, writing may give you some distraction. And e-coli??????!!! It would seem to me you've had more than your share. Not playing Job, are you? Will be holding you in my heart, as always and sending multiple virtual hugs.

I am looking forward to your letters. Let's get that damned book out in the world. Post-election, it needs it more than ever. My Boston friend sends anti-Trump things almost every day. Going to send you what she sent today—hopefully, it will make you giggle. Also I hope you have seen the last "Saturday Night Live"—I'd say it was about 85% Trump et al. It was quite hilarious.

Here, I'm madly beginning Mass Murders book[17]—sounding off so strongly in Chapter I, I wondered if my publisher might say he couldn't publish it. Then I thought, we have a contract! In the process, I found an interesting book, *American Psychosis* by a psychiatrist named E. Fuller Torrey (or maybe, it's the other way around), I never heard of him. He was at NIMH [National Institute of Mental Health] during the 60s etc. and is furious at the "failure" of well-intentioned mental health laws from then on. It's a history of mental health legislation from Kennedy's Community Mental Health act which led to the creation of Community Mental Health Centers, with all good intentions, planned to get psychiatric patients and others out of the back wards and into communities where they could be treated on an outpatient basis. I got into the biz just at that time and it's very confirming of the breakdown I have observed, spoken about and railed against for so many years. Reading the book, it was interesting to me that it was the ACLU who brought many cases about the rights of the mentally ill, especially their right to refuse treatment. I sure don't know what the answer is and remember hearing about

---

[17] *An art therapist considers mass murders, violence and mental illness.* Published by Charles C Thomas and due out about 2019.

the days when husbands committed their wife to the asylum for social control reasons, but it is virtually impossible these days to commit even a crazy person if they don't agree to treatment. If it can be proved they are a danger to self or others, they can be held for a few hours, but all therapists know this is very difficult to establish and I used to say, "there has to be blood on the steps to even have a chance." And a psychotic person in the middle of a psychotic episode doesn't think he is crazy–Catch 22. Ronald Reagan finished it off, of course, by closing the mental hospitals—first as California Governor, then as President. Fuller Torrey wrote Reagan didn't understand mental illness at all; he equated it with Communism. I was growing up in L.A. when he was the Screen Actors Guild President doing all that and the Writers Guild (which my father was part of) was fighting him. Ugggg.

Did I tell you, I'm going to LA for three days to see Alexa get the Humanitas Award?[18] I'll be very proud. But I

---

[18] Forty-two years old, the Humanitas Prize is for writing for movies and TV. As the program says "It honors film and television writers whose work explores the human condition in a nuanced, meaningful way...The overarching goal of Humanitas is to promote peace and love in the human family–one story at a time." My daughter was nominated for an episode she wrote for Netflix's series "Grace and Frankie" about assisted suicide.

am worried that you know who will close the National Science Foundation and Ben's Brazil grant will be gone.

And much love,

Max

Feb 7, 2017

Thanks, Max,

It has been a shitty five days. I am on meds that are supposed to stop the spreading. I started it today and take it for seven days–if I survive the side effects. The worst is the pain in my ear. But I'll take that as long as it doesn't travel up to my eye on that side.

I actually sorted out all of our letters today and just have a few that aren't printed out. Also, checked the Dropbox. I think they are duplicates of what I have on my computer.

I need all the hugs I can get. Out of isolation Thurs.

Love,

Myra

February, 18, 2017

Dear Max,

I am technically better–no more spots. I took all the medicine they gave me and feel like I've been on a marathon race.

Today, I finished making copies of all the letters/chapters I have on file for our book and in the Dropbox. I will mail all of this to you on Monday. I would like to interview a couple of men and a few couples. I want you to look over what I send (before you read seriously) and suggest something to send the publisher if she asks. I will also call her next week. We both have your notes, contents draft etc

I hope you are well.

Sent a letter to "New York Times." They will let me know if they will print it. I did not criticize Mrs. Pence[19]– just told the author of the article she didn't do her homework. Also asked what Mrs. Pence could do for us since The Trump administration doesn't support mental health care. Sick times.

Love, Myra

---

[19] Karen Pence, Vice President Mike Pence's wife, who said her cause would be art therapy, got a lot of art therapists riled up in opposition.

February 19, 2017

Darling,

Glad you are at least "technically" better from the shingles. I'm sure it's been no fun no matter what. You have been working nonetheless. Aren't you amazing! Looking forward to receiving the manuscript and getting to work on it. Here's the deal: Tuesday I go to LA for Alexa's Humanitas Award. Will be back late Thursday. I'll ask my renter to get the mail. But I probably will not be able to get to our book until next weekend. I'll have a look and get back to you. E.g. I know at one point I organized chapters. But later, I thought simply letters in chronological order. Let me see what I think when I see it all. Thanks so much for putting it together.

The American Art Therapy Association and everyone else has made the proper statements.[20] Now the question is will anyone do anything? (Like not embrace Pence) My guess is NO, as usual. And after the "uprising" it will go on the same way. Certainly the publicity couldn't hurt. I

---

[20] Karen Pence is Vice President Mike Pence's wife–in the Trump administration. She had said that her "cause" would be art therapy. There was a big rigmarole about this. I, (MBJ) resigned from the American Art Therapy Association and the Art Therapists for Social Rights Facebook page was established to further discussion and dissent. In 1969 Myra was a prime mover in the formation of the American Art Therapy Association, the professional organization for art therapists and she, naturally, retains a deep interest for her "creation."

wonder where conscience and integrity get into this at all? I certainly know where it *should*. Maybe I'll write that in some public forum. By the way, not only is the Trump administration against Medicare, it is against the NEA.

Love,

Max

March 4, 2017

Dearest Myra,

I am still working on going over what you sent and turning it into a manuscript. Probably will be for another few weeks. I'm into the emails from 2016 now. In the process, I am, of course, reading it–and I want you to know how GOOD I think it is and how much I love you–all over again. Our relationship, in and out of the book, has been extraordinarily valuable for me. I hold you in my heart, my dear, and always will.

Now off to pay bills!

Much love,

Max

March 4, 2017

Dear Max,

To say the feeling is mutual is an understatement and sounds trite. If the book is good, (and I think it is too,) it is because we are so connected in thoughts and feelings–open to new ideas and have a lovely openness in responding.

It has been a beautiful experience for me.

Take your time. I want to add more about my tablemates and I think this is a good place.

I love you too,

Myra

March 4, 2017 (continued)

Dear Max,

In a previous letter, I told you a little about the women I have had dinner with over the years. Obviously, in a community like this we lose friends and gain new ones. After several losses, Anne and I noticed Lorraine and Susan were sitting alone and we asked them if they would like to join us at dinner, making a table for four. It was a good decision and proved to be a pleasant and stimulating discussion every night. Moving into the presidential campaign, we discovered Anne was a liberal and a registered independent. No surprise, coming from this very bright lady who convened a history discussion here and conducted two on-going trivia games. One was during the day for individuals and the other, two evenings a month for teams. The three of us joined a team. Rose and Sheila were at another dinner table, but within the year asked to join us, making a table for six.

Anne was a long-time heavy smoker and suffered with severe COPD. She realized she was getting sicker and put herself on Hospice home care. She died soon after, a loss I and the women at our table did not recover from quickly. The church for Gay people that she had been a member of for many years, including some of the men who had become her close friends and whom I had met, made a beautiful memorial service that was what we all needed. Shortly before her death, she bet me $10 that Trump would win. I took her on and if and when we meet again, I owe her the money. We continued as a group of five.

A few months later, a new neighbor in the facility was introduced to me and Rose while we were in the card room waiting for our usual fourth player. Kate said she was a bridge player and joined us. We later asked if she would like to join our dinner table–filling the empty space Anne left.

Being close neighbors, Lorraine and I have probably come to know Kate better than the others at our table. It has been very hard for her to fit in and adjust. I must tell you: With Anne gone, I am the only one NOT from New York. Anne was from Chicago and I was born and raised in Philadelphia. Kate is just past 90 and was widowed 24 years ago. She has a son and his family in New York who she appears to be close to and a daughter she speaks very little of. She is beginning to have short-term memory problems, but is very bright, funny and still playing bridge. She was a yoga teacher and, frankly Max, walks and moves better than I did when I was seventy. But she is not happy here and doesn't want to "fit in." With all good intentions, of course, her son moved her here without giving her the opportunity to see it or other independent living communities. She is not the only one to be moved here by children. Having lived alone for so many years in an apartment complex, she cannot—and I suspect, will not—adjust to the schedules here or the daily routine. And apparently she can't make her own decision about where she lives!

Since Kate joined us, I have learned something very interesting: Growing up in New York doesn't mean you are "one of the New Yorkers"–a stereotype, I guess. There are those that have grown up in sections of the city that are considered more "acceptable" than others. Kate's background is very different from the other New York ladies at our table and she flaunts it. During the election campaign, some nights our dinner discussions would get very heated and we had to remind each other that one of the great things about America is free speech!

All this reminds me of Ellen whom I wrote about some months ago. Ellen came here shortly after being widowed. She had gone back to college in her mid-forties and was an Activities Therapist in a nursing home before she retired. While Ellen didn't sit with us or play bridge, I often sat and chatted with her. She replaced someone on the Resident Council and I worked with her there. But in less than a year, she left and moved to a condo community. She told me she could not tolerate the gossip at the dinner table. Both Kate and Ellen made me think of the article in the New York Times written by Jennifer Weiner, "Mean girls in the retirement home." Weiner cites a study that concludes "mean girls stay mean." I know Kate has experienced "this meanness" and I imagine Ellen did too.

I have been here for over five years and had only one encounter with such a "mean girl." I have managed to steer clear of her and noticed that she sadly, often eats alone. I think meanness is comparatively rare here and I believe it is because most of us, men and women, find a place for ourselves here and do fit in.

Love,

Myra

March 7, 2017

Dear Myra,

Your letter describing your friends and tablemates at your community fascinated me and set me thinking about a number of things. So here goes. First, I got envious: To have a ready-made group of friends so easily available seems quite ideal. Then I got to thinking about the woman who left, not liking the gossip, and the "mean girl" statements. I wonder if I could be flexible enough to adjust to that; I know logically, it's to be expected in a community like yours where there are lots of different kinds of people with different backgrounds and experiences.

I actually don't mind gossip. It's endless surface and "stupid" conversation I'm not interested in. Sometimes I even get exasperated and lose patience about the lack of sophistication here where I live. I have to talk to myself and remind myself that that's the way it is. Either accept it or move–and I'm not going to move. It passes.

The conversations that went on in my parents' living room caused me to be virtually non-verbal as I grew up because I thought I didn't have anything smart to say (I didn't notice that those conversations I heard were by very smart grownup people, writers and directors, and not a kid like me.) I remember in elementary school, each student had to recite a poem about the parts of speech. I hung back, terribly fearful, was the last one and almost didn't get through it at all. (It's one of the reasons I got into art.) I could certainly talk one on one and in small groups, but larger groups terrified me and things like (what we had then) "cocktail parties" were very difficult and often I simply stayed silent. I told myself that by the time I was 21, I would be able to speak easily. I got to 21 and couldn't, so I moved the time to 29. Couldn't then either, but eventually found something worth speaking about, "Operation Adventure" my arts program in the poor communities of San Diego. So, I opened my mouth and, with a lot of preparation, gave– speeches to the Eagles, Mooses, and etc. As a more than 30-year teacher and academic, speaking is still not easy for me. It isn't, I have discovered, easy for most women who have little training and usually are not given much experience during their early life, not to mention that their higher voices than men, sometimes don't carry or sound "commanding."

In the last ten years or so of living here, I have noticed that as they get older, many people are more reticent and do not venture out as much, myself included. Obsession with attending a multitude of external events and etc. seem to recede. For example, our uninstructed drawing group which was started by an old friend and myself and meets for life drawing weekly in a yurt has been going now for nine years. Many of the people in it have been there for the whole time and the nine years is a timeframe of people growing older. The group is a working group in which we also talk with each other about all kinds of things including the happenings of the day. (One person says she comes for the conversation and also draws a bit.) We have a model and accept people who are beginners at drawing and those that are really pros. What we don't have is any instruction.

As an organizer of the group, I noticed that things have changed in our nine years, like people's memories and I have to do a lot more reminding of this or that. Some people get things quite mixed up. Every year when asked about continuing, 100% want to. One man said he wanted to sign up for five years. I suspect it's a lot like your dinner table conversations. It happens to be a fascinating group of fairly bright and informed people. We've had a lot come to the group, stay for a while and leave for one reason or another. One person left because it wasn't structured enough for him and we resisted when he tried to structure it more tightly. This wasn't what was said, of course–but this is what it was. He was used to controlling things and liked it that way. It is predominantly women with a few men. (Wanting to attend the group, one man asked "are those hens still there?") We have heard the rumor that we vet an applicant's art and you've got to be very proficient to get in–absolutely untrue.

A number of people here are readying their house for sale and planning to move to an Independent Living facility in the next years. I guess older driving is a big problem and I hear of many who shouldn't, still driving. What I don't often hear about are car accidents (although my daughter, age 50, was stopped here by a cop for driving too slowly!) Particularly for men, I know that giving up driving is very difficult because it is often the last bastion of control against growing old. One of my neighbors became too old to drive and I used to see the cab outside his house a lot waiting for him. There are also local programs with drivers who will drive you places, but of course, this involves asking–hard for some, hard for me. I haven't liked to drive at night for a few years and I have two friends who will come get me and take me to the movies. So I believe that one of the necessities of growing older is learning to be vulnerable, even dependent at times, and being able to ask for help.

But yesterday the local founder of the aging in place program, in response to an announcement I sent her, wrote me "Congratulations for not retiring." I wrote back "To paraphrase Gloria Steinem, this IS what retirement looks like these days." It made me think of the prevailing, outdated definitions of "retirement."

Another necessity is meals. I have never been much of a cook, nor do I enjoy the process, but I have noticed that to even cook up stir fry now is sometimes too much. I am tied to my microwave and my pbj sandwiches, which I quite like. But must admit it might be nice to have that all taken care of. Not now, but maybe in the future.

And my company? My sweet Havanese dog, Betsy, who follows me everywhere. Right now she is curled up at my feet on her little rug. Her bed is mine–I call hers "The Princess Betsy Pillow" and it is very comforting to wake up in the middle of the night and see her sweet black and white haired body next to me. She is a good companion without noise or opinions. Sweet and cuddly, but no demands. On her trips out with Eve and the big dogs for exercise, I say she has a secret life she doesn't tell me anything about. The questions and discussions continue in my head without stimulation from my environment.

I want to tell you about an experience I had a few days ago that I have been mulling over. I went to the local minimart to pick up something and checking out, had the following conversation with the checker. Now, I must add that I know the cashier by sight but have never had anything other than small talk with him. He said "How's your day going?" I replied "Fine so far. How's yours?" "I can't complain." Then he went on to tell me a very sad story about how his storage facility was broken into and all his things from his dead father, including his father's ashes, had been stolen. "No complaints?" He thanked me for listening.

Living alone as I do, is right for me now. But I could envision being in a facility some years down the line (I turn 80 this summer) I can see it would be nice to have the necessities close by and to be able to feel safe and taken care of. I surely hope when that time comes that I will still be flexible enough to tolerate and be kind to what I'm sure are the silly rules and even some silly people.

Love,

Max

April 15, 2017

Dear Max,

Winding down on Passover and revving up on finishing our book. One grandson and family at Bonnie's house gone this morning and Bonnie and Joel are catching their breath. Karen's stepdaughter and family and more of Marvin's family here all week, including his brother and nephews from Miami. Since my contribution was giving them recipes and checking on results, I am now home and ready to go to work on the book. It was hectic, but wonderful–especially with all the small and young children.

I really like our book, Max, and hope others will enjoy it and even learn something from it. My daughters read a few chapters before the holidays (when Marsha was here,) loved it and are psyched to write a collaborative Foreword. I hope you had a happy holiday and are feeling good. I am finally feeling much better and having whole days without pain. Shingles is definitely not for old people. But then, neither is old age.

Love,

Myra

April 17, 2017

Dear Myra,

I am sure glad your Shingles have calmed down. Who needs that!

And your description of your whole family for Passover made me nostalgic. As very non-traditional secular Jews, the Seder dinner was the only Jewish tradition in our family year after year, although they were largely attended by non-Jews (which, as you know, is also the tradition.) Those dinners were held each year through my childhood and then through my children's generation. I remember them as being hilarious and my then five-year-old brother getting drunk on Manischevitz [kosher wine.] When it said "drink the first cup of wine," he did–the whole thing. Our Haggadah[21] was written by Mrs. Rabbi

---

[21] "Reading the Hagaddah at the Seder table is a fulfillment to each Jew to "tell your son of the Jewish liberation from slavery in Egypt as described in the Book of Exodus in the [sic] Torah." Retrieved April 17, 2017 from Wikipedia>wiki/Hagaddah_of_Pesach.

Somebody and was so stilted and hard to read that we all laughed at it. But reading it over all those years we came to feel a strong affection toward it, like a weird but present relative. I remember that Rosie, the Davies' maid cooked the dinner and we always had the first strawberries of the season.

Since I have been on Whidbey Island, I have looked for community Seders, but found very little. Jews don't seem to have infiltrated the Pacific Northwest much, and on Whidbey Island, I have felt that to say you are a Jew is a little like it used to be for Gays—a coming out of the closet almost.

The first year I was here, I found a Seder dinner given at a local community center. I invited a few non-Jewish friends and hoped for a good evening. But entering the hall, the rabbi–who was also a guitar player–was playing the Seder songs to the "Sound of Music." I didn't think that was a good omen (and it wasn't.) A few years ago, the Whidbey Jews put on a Seder service. We were told to each bring cutlery and a plate and a long table was set diagonally in the upstairs community room. About 40 people, Jews of every persuasion sat around it. It was announced that the Haggadah has been read by a committee and everything removed that might be objectionable including the word "Egypt." I was shocked–Jews are known for being direct, forthright and even objectionable. And how could you tell the Seder story without the word "Egypt?" At that point, I decided my days of trying to find a regular Seder service might be over. I tried once again last year when I was invited by a friend. They had been cooking for days and the food was wonderful, but it was as if that was enough and there was no reading of the Haggadah and the Seder service to go with it. I gave up, which may be just as well, and I live with my memories of the "old" days.

Love, Max

April 30, 2017

Dear Myra,

I found your discussion of the people you know and the dinners at your facility fascinating. It is so different from what I am used to. I wonder if you think "dressing up" of your cohorts is generational? Or could it be that it is the custom in your facility? Or is it Florida?

I have found it so different in a small town in Washington state than I did in Los Angeles. Many people move here upon retirement and the look is "natural. That means there is probably more grey hair here than elsewhere–certainly than in L.A. A full-house at the local movie theater, the Clyde, means a theater 98% full of grey-haired people. (I'm not sure if it is undyed, but it sure is grey.) I have a friend who jokes that she and I are the only ones who don't look old because she dyes her hair brown and I dye mine pretty red now. For me, it's not to look young, but because I like it that way. But grey hair remains a code for old. Actually, a person of my age who doesn't have grey hair here, sticks out. Someone who wore a lot of makeup and eye shadow would stick out here too. In L.A. that would be just one of the crowd.

As to "dressing up": Even in the fanciest restaurants we've got here, it is very informal, often not even clean. To look like you cleaned up and dressed for dinner, for example, is seldom done, if at all. When I first got here, I went to dinner with some friends. I wore a fairly ordinary top and some jeans and they laughed at me and told me what a city person I looked like! Nobody wears any kind of heels and a long time ago, when I tried to buy a pair for a wedding, I couldn't. Women here still pay attention to having their nails, and sometimes toe nails, manicured and painted. I have never done that and I don't do that now.

When I ask about "generation," it is because I think mine was the first to experience and be part of the second wave women's movement, which had a lot to say about how women looked and were objectified. (Remember the Miss America stuff?) We were the bra burners and the ones who got rid of girdles (although Spanks are simply a later incarnation of girdles.) Pacific Northwest women dress in neutral colors and black. Kind of a "not being seen" quality about it. Not like New Yorkers and black as a sophisticated color. To wear color here is to be unusual, whereas in Los Angeles, of course, it was the usual. Might have something to do with the weather, but certainly not just that.

You remember I was at Loyola Marymount University for about 25 years. In academia in L.A., women could wear whatever they wanted, although it was the time of suits and briefcases in many professions. I had a lot of wearable art clothes and enjoyed dressing as a creative act.

My mother was absolutely uninterested in clothes, except for covering her body, despite her having been a theatrical costume designer; She had what she called her "uniforms." She even had a sewing machine that didn't work, so I never learned to sew at all, even when I wanted to, because the sewing machine in our house was so frustrating.

I have gotten rid of most of my delicious wearable art clothes that I treasured. To wear them here is simply not done. I have kept a few pieces because I couldn't bear to give them away I loved them so much, but I don't get much chance ever to wear them. Here, I am known to "dress differently" simply because I pay attention sometime to pattern and design. But I don't do it for anybody but myself and never have. It was always for my own pleasure.

I dyed my hair deep red about 25 years ago. I hung out for two weeks at a beauty salon near my house in Mendocino doing a photographic essay (that I later exhibited.) At the end of the project, I decided I wanted to dye my hair. They didn't know how to do it in that salon, so we figured it out together. When I moved to Whidbey, the salon nearest my home happened to be owned by a man who had been a colorist in Orange County, California, so he knows how and I just kept doing it. It covers up the grey, for sure.

Way back, in Los Angeles, when I was first married and with a new baby and feeling overwhelmed with responsibility, I would have done anything to get out of the house for a while and have someone take care of me. I went to the nearest beauty salon on Santa Monica Boulevard and got my hair done. When finished, I said I wanted to come back about every six weeks. The male stylist said "Why?" But then he said: "The next time you come in, I'll twirl your ends." I wasn't sure what he meant by that, but I never went back.

Love,

Max

May 1, 2017

Dear Max,

I think the dressing up for dinner IS generational and the rule here. No shorts are allowed in the dining room for dinner. Remember we are in Florida. Residents may dress any way they like for breakfast and lunch–and they do. I generally have my breakfast and lunch on my patio, overlooking a huge lake. I love it and am very disappointed on the rare bad weather days. When I get dressed, it is for the day and that is true for many others.

When I was visiting places with Bonnie to move to, we were always invited to lunch and learned the dress code was like this one. Initially, men were not allowed to wear hats for dinner here, but because some men and women have eye problems and are disturbed by the overhead lights, that rule has been cancelled. We have some women here that actually wear lovely, wide-brimmed hats all day.

The majority of women and men here do have either gray or (beautiful) white hair. Very few color their hair, but there are gorgeous blond wigs on several 90+ residents. I suspect that there are more toupees than I know of, and I think the men are just as vain as the women. I have had a number of women and men stop me to ask who "streaks my hair?" My answer, of course, is always Mother Nature and it appears that, so far, she has treated me well.

Love,

Myra

May 1, 2017

Dear Myra,

I have wondered about the impact of "loss of looks," particularly for women, as one grows older. The culture is so youth oriented and demanding about how a woman should look and, indeed, shaming if they don't look that way. I suspect this "loss" may be more difficult than increasing body fragility and problems. I have a friend who was considered very beautiful when she was young and got a lot of attention for that. As she ages, she has become "invisible" and she is having a terrible time.

As a young girl, I never thought myself pretty. I was not the stereotypical, acceptable blue-eyed wasp blond. From an early age, about ten, I thought I weighed too much, which unfortunately is not an atypical story for girls. The media and environment pounded me with this message. At best, I was called then "interesting looking." And we all know what that means—certainly I did. That's what I was alright, but "unusual" simply didn't fit in.

When I look back at the few photographs of me then, I was quite beautiful, but in an "interesting" and unusual way. Like most other women I spent a lifetime trying to lose weight, filling my thoughts with worry and guilt and often feeling deprived. I lived in Los Angeles after all, which may have made it worse.

In the first weeks I came to Whidbey Island 16 years ago (I was 65,) I was invited to a birthday party. It was all women who spent most of the party time talking about their weight—how too much it was and their multiple attempts at trying to solve their never-ending problem. I was shocked at this and there and then determined to no longer give that issue time and space in my life or psyche.

A few years ago, when the image looking back at me from the mirror began to look like my mother and somebody I didn't know, I decided to give up mirrors. (I actually suggest this idea to older people.) The person I felt inside was full of energy, ideas and youth. The person I saw in the mirror was "old." How could I reconcile these two Selfs? I still have one mirror above my bathroom sink, to brush my teeth, comb my hair and put on my makeup–but that's all. I have no others and consciously resist checking my reflection in other places, like in the shower door.

The result for me has been a resolution where I feel much younger–about 15 usually–without a wrinkly image to contradict my sense of myself and remind me that I'm not.

Love,

Max

AFTER THOUGHTS

May 28, 2017

Dear Max,

As you know, I recently reviewed our whole manuscript on the aging process, and I must say, we covered a lot of ground, spewed some words of wisdom, some words of angst, many words of love and some words of distress. I also realized I mentioned some things briefly that need elaborating and you asked some questions I did not fully respond to. So here goes.

The death of my friend Ann was a real loss for me. She was my partner in preparing and conducting the Women's Club luncheons and she helped me write the Resident Council by-laws; together we started a movie/book club and planned to take over editing the "Round Table Resident Journal" when I finished my term on the Council. The Women's Club luncheons were a huge success and many women here want to know when they will be held again. They were stopped temporarily due to renovations. The mañana mentality in Florida makes every undertaking move slowly.

The movie/book club lasted less than a year. The Activities Director was most supportive, helping to get copies of the books and the movies we wanted. But the discussion of the comparison of movie to the book was poorly attended and Ann and I ended up talking to each other and only a few others. I have concluded that most of this generation of oldies is not into "taking part" in a discussion that requires preparation–like reading the book and, maybe, staying up a half hour longer. They want to be entertained–unless they were that non-conforming woman who worked or that unusual man who pursued intellectual interests outside of making a living.

The by-laws have been amended only twice in four years and are good. But the story of the Resident Council is rather startling–and I believe another example of how this new generation of seniors responds to crisis. Jean was elected president, I was Secretary, a member who was completing her 4th year here was Vice President. The other four members were eligible to be re-elected. Jean died suddenly after two months in office, and the remainder of the year was difficult. When it ended, everyone on the Council eligible to run for office resigned. Max, there were then over 150 residents here in Independent Living and only four chose to submit resumes for office. The by-laws require seven members so there is no Residents Council now. Our Executive Director and management staff were dumbfounded, and so was I. Our Executive Director checked around and this lack of participation appears to be a new happening in this kind of senior community. And no one knows what to do about it. The staff now conducts monthly meetings where residents can ask questions, make suggestions and complain. But a significant and informed group of liaisons to management as was the Resident Council no longer exists.

But keeping my promise to Ann, the first issue of the new "Round Table Journal" was delivered April 1. I have three co-editors, proof reading and helping with layout. The Activities Director prints copies for the community. With support and enthusiasm from executive staff, I have expanded the journal to include submissions from the staff and invite a resident or staff artist to submit one of their own art creations for the cover. Our first issue was a huge success and as I write this, we are preparing the Summer issue. We plan four issues a year. The "wanna be" writers and artists are coming out of hiding.

A young staff person here submitted a "Sonnet for Her Grandmother" to our journal. She told me our generation has so much wisdom to impart and "she loves working here and listening" to us. We can't ask for more than this.

On a solemn note, when you asked me how I managed [my husband] Len's death, I wrote that at his funeral I read his ethical will. I also told you I had included it in a memory book I made for my children and grandchildren. I am delighted that it has become a "coffee table book" for them and the impact his enclosed will has already made on some future decisions has stunned and delighted me. I have realized there are very few people that know what an ethical will is. So for our uninformed readers, I want to give a brief history and definition. I first learned about Ethical Wills in the early 1970s at a workshop for memoir writing sponsored by the National League of American Pen Women. This kind of will cites no monetary value of objects generally listed in regular last will and testament documents. The author of an Ethical Will describes his or her values, beliefs, ideals and urges those left behind to live their lives the way he or she did. The first published Ethical Will was written by Thomas Jefferson.

Later, I found a book about Jewish Ethical Wills written by Rabbi Jack Reimer, whom I knew personally. Len was as intrigued as I with the idea of such a will and told me I was to write one. We had a little disagreement about this and I did not write one. But unbeknownst to any of us, he did, in 1976, and I found it with his living will when he was last hospitalized.

The following three vignettes reflect not only do we have something to say, but that our grandchildren, and the younger generation want to hear from us. A year after Len died my oldest great grandson, Ben then 9, announced he wanted to go to Hebrew School and have a Bar Mitzah. My granddaughter-in-law is the child of a Christian mother and Jewish father and with my grandson, celebrated all the holidays from both faiths. They were surprised at this early request, impressed with their son's making his own decisions and promptly enrolled him in a Hebrew school nearby. The following year I was invited to stay at their new home over Thanksgiving and the morning after Ben told me he and his mother wanted to show me something. The "something" was an essay he had written for an assignment from Hebrew School. The children were asked to write about what their family considered holy. He and his mom agreed that while Len's Will was not holy, it was revered by the family. This was the subject of his essay and he quoted Len's statement "to honor your roots and live by its' principles and values." I was overwhelmed, as, I was told his teachers were, who had never heard of an Ethical Will. And we all realized this was the source of Ben's request to study for Bar Mitzvah. Another grandchild considering marriage told me they had dwelled on "Pop pop's" Will and his statement that "who you marry is the most important decision of your life."

This is a story you have part of in my career memoir, published in your book, *Architects of Art Therapy,* so I will be brief here. In one of your letters you talked about the Mental Health Act and how it created havoc in the Mental Health field on the West Coast. Instead of improving care for mentally ill patients, it created a whole new community of homeless people. The Act was adopted in Pennsylvania around 1963, while I was still working on the psychiatric unit at Albert Einstein Medical Center. In 1966, the brilliant young director of our unit, Morris Goldman, was offered the position of Director of the new Mental Health Community Center at Hahnemann Medical College and Hospital in center city, Philadelphia. These centers were opened in strategic places in the city and this particular one was considered Number 1, serving the largest area of indigent neighborhoods and high-rise luxury apartments. It was a position Dr. Goldman could not afford to pass up. You do know that subsequently, he convinced the Dean of the Graduate School to start an art therapy program there, and while he would be named Director of that program, I would be in charge. Curriculum development and course credits were not in his repertoire. Within a few months after his appointment, I and some of the nursing staff became an integral part of that facility. I had a front seat watching patients from the (then) shut-down state hospital, released, put in boarding houses in center city and assigned to our Day Hospital, for medication and a treatment plan. Some of these people had been hospitalized for decades; they didn't know how to navigate travel on the subway or make their way through a supermarket. A program was established that invited older people (then 60 to 75 years) living in that area, to be "enablers." They served as resource people and were available to, literally, teach how to live in the real world. They were supervised by a professional mental health worker. I remember my mother and stepfather volunteered and my mother told me one of the women assigned to them had no idea where to buy a bra or how to travel on a trolley car. That was a very good program. But we also learned that the "landlords" of the boarding houses were sadly not helping these patients manage their social security checks–they were often stealing them. As you know, the "new" program for mental health care soon fell apart, and over 50 years later we are lacking in care of the mentally ill.

When I think back to that horror and see the growth and longevity of our population today, I know we are lucky that someone thought of senior communities. While they are far from perfect and still need a lot of learning, they are keeping many old people from living alone, living in a community where there is help for problems that may emerge–from physical illness to depression and other manifestations of aging, is not a bad thing.

You did ask me if I thought the women here worried about losing their looks as they aged. Max: I don't know anyone here that got rid of all their mirrors. You are amazing. But from my perspective the women here, regardless of age, are very attentive to their appearance, including me. Shorts are not allowed at dinner, for women and men. Generally, the women dress in attractive to beautiful tops, nice pants and most wear makeup. We have a beauty salon on the premises and I know many women go weekly to have their hair and nails done. I go every week to have my hair washed, simply because I have trouble lifting my arms up. But I do style it myself. There are several women I know who have standing appointments in outside salons and arrange for transportation–which is most accommodating here. So. Yes, I do think they worry about losing their looks. For the most part, they make every effort to look well dressed and well-coiffed. Maybe that is a big difference between living alone and living in a community of peers. While some of us take losing our looks as "par for the course," we do "dress up" for dinner.

My story regarding thoughts about my own looks, goes back to when I was twelve. It was my birthday and my parents were taking me to a well-known Chinese restaurant in center city. I remember my mother allowed me to put on a little lipstick. As we were walking to get the trolley we came abreast of a neighbor sitting outside. After exchanging greetings, he told my parents I was growing up to be a beautiful young lady. My father promptly told him it was as important to be beautiful on the inside as it was on the outside. It was not until I was in my 30s, Max, working on the psychiatric unit, that I allowed myself to accept a complement on my looks. One of the psychiatrists on the unit complimented me on how I looked that day. I barely said "thank you" and looked very uncomfortable. He asked me what my problem was – and I told him the story of my father's response when I was twelve. He told me it was time to "grow up." I, too, dress up for dinner, wear nice clothes, use make up and when told I look nice, say "thank you".

Before I close, I want to tell you about a little ritual my tablemates and I share most nights. Five of us all live in the same building and take the same elevator to our apartments after dinner, except on those nights when there is entertainment in the auditorium. When we are on the elevator with our walkers, there is no room for anyone else. Rose is the first to get off and as she leaves, she will say "See you tomorrow, God willing." I do know that we all have different beliefs, but for some reason, we all smile, even laugh and echo her words– "God willing." I have no idea where this came from or who started it. But I would like to end my letters here with the hope that we both live long enough to see our words published and that those that should, listen and improve this safe harbor for the future aging generations to come. God willing.

With love, a long distance hug and much appreciation for sharing this journey with me,

Myra

June 10, 2017

Dear Myra,

It seems strange to be writing a "last" letter; I'm glad we will continue writing to each other. I am loathe to let you go. Perhaps we will do a Volume II?

I have the "Little Cottage"–a fisherman's cottage brought up from the beach, they say– on my property which I rent out. My current renter, Rose, is leaving with her pet bunnies to stay with her mother on the mainland who is sick and lives in an apartment alone. The mother is on oxygen and when the power goes off, which it often does in these winters, Rose has to go off the island on the ferry to her mother's to take care of it.

I remember that my renter before Rose, who was here for a number of years, left to stay with her elderly father in Walla Walla. It does not escape my notice that both my renters are women and both are single. Should this caretaking be considered an actual life stage task these days for living alone? Does it mean that, at a certain point, your daughter–if you've got one and maybe if she's single–may come to live with you? The younger generation is often called the "sandwich generation" meaning that first you take care of your children and then you take care of your parents. I wonder?

Myra, you are an important role model for me; you have brought into bright light that there are vast differences between *caretaking and living*. Although some of your grown children reside near you, you refused to live with them but continue to *live a life of your own choosing that is created and managed by YOU.* It has in it the new friends and activities *you* want. Admirable, I'd say.

I think you have underscored the difference between being passive and dependent and being active and independent in later life. Caretaking as it becomes necessary for you will be assumed by the facility, not by your children. My adorable son said I could come live with him. Myra: Your example proves that an older person's increasing physical fragility and their mental and emotional "well-being" are different things and must be considered differently.

Some years ago, when I had my left hip replaced, I was sent to a rehab facility for a week. I understood that this was necessary because I live alone and didn't have someone to take care of me at home. Along with the rehab section, this old hospital functioned as an assisted living/skilled nursing facility. It was pretty horrifying. I remember that even the physical environment was dark, drab and impersonal. It would be hard to imagine that if you were not depressed when you got there, you would be very soon in a world where passivity and waiting were the central acceptable values. It looked like dying was about the only independent act left.

Obviously, not all facilities are like this, but that you, after Len died, picked the one where you live especially because *they asked you what YOU want,* is so right. That they asked you was a clue that they recognized that their clients are (still) *functioning, active human beings with wants and desires.*

We live in a culture with rampant Ageism, where, all-too-often older people are thought to disappear into increasing needlessness and nothing where the best thing that can be done is to kindly care for them until the end. A lot of people and a lot of facilities seem to do just that, but you and I know too many feisty, alive elders to believe that is true for all. We *are* some of those alive people!

I want to live as long as I can. I want to live until I die. There is plenty of help around to die—with dignity and everything else. Depending on when and how, I may have to swallow my independent nature a bit and accept whatever caretaking I need. But as an older person, I may need help to live!

A major theme of our book is that serious education and training is necessary to work with older people and unfortunately, it is rare so far. But it's not just book learning that is necessary. Who is best to give that education? Us. We can be the sources of the finest kind of information there is—the kind that comes from human experience, from living and living through a life filled with trauma and pleasures. There are plenty of 75+ in the United States to ask and to listen to. For all the complexities and nuances of older life, you don't get it till you get there—good intentions notwithstanding. And when you get it, you have an important and universal human story. It is a story that *should* be told and that the generations need to hear.

Another central theme of this book is that the emotional and mental life of seniors needs sensitive and steady attending to, along with the physical. It's not like your marbles evaporate at a certain age. Physical decomposition can be widely recognized–it often is visible, for one thing, but not so much emotional needs. In my view, each elder community should have a regular consultant who would see to individual and community emotional needs and well-being. I dislike tooting my own horn, or those of my profession, but it seems to me that art therapy might be particularly useful here: First, a person creates something physical that has important meaning to the person and to their family. But the object has an on-going physical life as well. (As you know Myra, this is exactly what your resident/staff journal is about.) In a facility, these art pieces could be collected into a book which remains on a shelf for community use and becomes a concrete visual symbol of all who have lived here. I very much like the idea of integrating residents and staff because it is a recognition that regardless of age, human beings have been here and have contributed. And that their contributions live on.

Finally, we come to the huge issue of *loss*. As Erickson no doubt would say, it is a consistent task of the older life stage. But is it something that the older person simply has to bear or might there be some better ways to both acknowledge the loss–some very profound and sad– and still recognize that life goes on? The AIDS quilt is an important recognition of loss and going on. I am fond of the quote from Fritz Stern at the beginning of this book: "Every loss diminishes one's life–and somehow redoubles one's responsibility."

Much love,

Max

ACKNOWLEDGEMENTS

Our first thanks go to the myriad of friends and neighbors who supported the idea of this book with enthusiasm, usually noting that there was nothing like it already. They gave us their stories, opinions (of which they had many) and finally, quotations about aging with openness, appreciation and urgency.

We thank our wonderful children for their Forewords, in which we found a sensitive and moving understanding of us and our work seldom spoken of between children and their mothers.

Benjamin Junge was Max's ever-present and speedy computer backup and took the photo for her author's picture.

Ahna Dunn-Wilder designed the book and shepherded it to publishing with a rare attention to detail and an artist's eye. Ahna also designed the cover and Myra Levick painted the cover picture of the tree.

ABOUT THE AUTHORS

Myra F. Levick

By her daughters:

From our earliest memories, our mother was <u>leading</u>: PTA President, Brownie Troop and Girl Scout Leader, Temple Sisterhood President. From elementary school forward, our friends and their parents took note: No card playing, golf or weekly trips to the hair salon. In her spare time, she painted and colored her own hair.

When we were 7, 8 and 10 years old, she became a college student. She earned a BFA in painting, an M.Ed. and a Ph.D. in Psychology. A painter, she persuaded a couple of innovative psychiatrists on an in-patient psychiatric unit to consider how art might aid them in understanding and treating their patients. From that experiment at a hospital in Philadelphia, the nascent field of Art Therapy acquired a bold champion. Our mother helped found the American Art Therapy Association, developed the first graduate curriculum in the country in Art Therapy and pioneered the integration of music and dance therapy into a comprehensive creative arts program. She wrote a textbook to guide the education of these new recruits and other books followed.

Myra's professional biography is exceptional, but her personal journey is no less so. As a career woman finding her way in the 1960s, she embodied both "Mad Men" and *The Feminine Mystique* simultaneously. She was a feminist before "Ms. Magazine" published its first issue, a lived example of the power of women before the modern battles to win passage of the Equal Rights Amendment unfolded and unraveled in the 1970s and early 80s. She moved in a male-dominated professional milieu, ignoring the historic barriers to women playing in the medical and health sciences sandbox.

As children, we were at times confused: She worked when none of our friends' mothers worked. She was busy when our friends' mothers were free. She was dressed when our friends' mothers were casual. But as we matured into young women ourselves, we understood the courage of her choices, the brilliance of her mind, and the priceless gift of leadership, power and equality that she bestowed on us. As children we may have dwelled on the empty seat in the school auditorium, but as women we learned to marvel at the richness of her legacy. As her daughters, we learned how to come of age in America.

Maxine Borowsky Junge

Born and raised in Los Angeles, Max moved to Whidbey Island, Washington 16 years ago after retirement from Loyola Marymount University where she was faculty member and Chair of the Marital and Family Therapy/Clinical Art Therapy Department. She has also taught at Immaculate Heart College, Goddard College and Antioch University. She is a psychotherapist, art psychotherapist and maintained a private practice in Los Angeles for many decades. She has written 10 books mostly about art therapy and creativity. Her latest book before this one is *Voices from the Barrio, the story of "Con Safos: Reflections of Life in the Barrio.* "Con Safos" was the first ever independent Chicano literary magazine; it was published in the late 1960s, early 1970s in East Los Angeles.

Her essay on Gilbert Magu Luján has recently been printed in the monograph *From Aztlán to Magulandia* which accompanies the retrospective exhibit of his artwork at the University of California at Irvine.

On Whidbey, Max makes art (latest series on mass murders,) writes, does yoga, reads, goes to the movies, consults and teaches psychotherapists and students, and sees friends for nurturing conversation. Her folk art collection keeps growing and gives her great pleasure. She has stopped driving at night.

Max's interest in aging springs from her own increasing years and the realization that the expanding numbers of older people in the United States are virtually an invisible and unrecognized population and are often discriminated against. She believes ageism is a serious problem and would be happy to email with anyone who wants to write at MBJunge@whidbey.net